The True Secret
of Writing

ALSO BY NATALIE GOLDBERG

MEMOIR
Long Quiet Highway: Waking Up in America
Living Color: A Writer Paints Her World
The Great Failure: My Unexpected Path to Truth

POETRY
Chicken and in Love
Top of My Lungs: Poems and Paintings

WRITING BOOKS
Writing Down the Bones: Freeing the Writer Within
Wild Mind: Living the Writer's Life
Thunder and Lightning: Cracking Open the Writer's Craft
Old Friend from Far Away: The Practice of Writing Memoir

NOVEL
Banana Rose

NOTEBOOK
The Essential Writer's Notebook

DOCUMENTARY FILM
Tangled Up in Bob: Searching for Bob Dylan
(with filmmaker Mary Feidt)

The True Secret of Writing

Connecting Life with Language

NATALIE GOLDBERG

ATRIA BOOKS

New York   London   Toronto   Sydney   New Delhi

ATRIA BOOKS

A Division of Simon & Schuster, Inc.
1230 Avenue of the Americas
New York, NY 10020

First Atria Books hardcover edition March 2013

ATRIA B O O K S and colophon are trademarks of Simon & Schuster, Inc.

For information about special discounts for bulk purchases, please contact Simon
& Schuster Special Sales at 1-866-506-1949 or business@simonandschuster.com

The Simon & Schuster Speakers Bureau can bring authors to your live event. For
more information or to book an event contact the Simon & Schuster Speakers
Bureau at 1-866-248-3049 or visit our website at www.simonspeakers.com.

Designed by Maura Fadden Rosenthal /Mspace

Permission credits appear on page 235–236

Manufactured in the United States of America

10   9   8   7   6   5   4   3   2   1

Library of Congress Cataloging-in-Publication Data
Goldberg, Natalie.
The true secret of writing: connecting life with language / Natalie Goldberg.
p. cm.
1. English language—Rhetoric—Study and teaching. 2. Creative writing—Study
and teaching.
I. Title.
PE1408.G5733 2012
808'.042—dc23   2012024961

ISBN: 978-1-4516-4124-0
ISBN: 978-1-4516-4126-4(ebook)

In memory of Katherine Thanas (1927–2012)
Zen teacher
Friend
still so much to say

Contents

◆ ◆ ◆

PART THREE

Elaborations

PART FOUR

Encounters and Teachers

Introduction

◆　◆　◆

A DECADE AGO, when I initially came up with the title "The True Secret of Writing," it was a bit tongue-in-cheek. I've used that phrase when a student has come late to class: "Oh, Sheila, I'm so sorry. You just missed it—a moment ago I told the students the true secret of writing. I am only able to utter it every five years or so." I'm teasing, but it gets the point across—be on time. This is your moment. Don't miss it.

Of course, no one possesses the one single true secret. If someone says he does, run for the hills. It's a dangerous idea. Life is not a commodity and is not singular but full of diversity.

For the past twelve years I have held weeklong retreats at the Mabel Dodge Luhan House in Taos, New Mexico, titled "The True Secret," where we practice sitting meditation, slow walking, and writing throughout the day. People come because they want to write, but over the years I've realized that it's not just writing that they want. They want connection; a spiritual longing drives them, a groping for meaning. Maybe they once read a single book—*Diary of Anne Frank, Leaving Cheyenne, The Brothers Karamazov*—that shattered them and they can't forget it. Or they desire to speak the truth to their fathers. They want this connection through language, through words on a page. Other methods exist—tai chi, yoga, Tibetan Buddhism, retreats in nature—but their yearning manifests through writing. It also encompasses something larger than writing—after all, they could have gone to a creative writing program that so many colleges and universities offer.

I've extended these retreats to other places, Omega Institute in New York, Hollyhock in Canada, Upaya Zen Center and Vallecitos

Mountain Refuge in New Mexico—under different titles. But the ones at Mabel's are the model, my base for experiment, my home lab.

Over these many continuous years a rhythm has been established at Mabel's and, with this repetition, I have been able to study the mechanical bones that best make up the week. The structure is easily applicable in other situations: to one full day, an hour in a public school class, or an afternoon at home. Individuals or a group of even two or three people can use it. Ultimately, you want to internalize this structure, so you carry it inside you, as a way to sustain and connect with your life.

I have been a Zen practitioner for many years so I naturally modified and modeled the writing retreats from the basic structure of formal Zen retreats. The True Secret is backed by a two-thousand-year-old tradition of practice. It is not simply a creative idea that Natalie, an individual, came up with willy-nilly. It's the practice of a Western woman in her time and culture meeting head-on the masterminds of ancient Eastern Zen wisdom. And voilà—something fresh, yet rooted, has evolved.

Make no mistake: the practice in this book is not limited to any sect or religion or creative urge. It's for everyone, and it can feed and enrich whatever religion, occupation, bent of mind, or situation you find yourself in.

The one important element that I have added to a traditional meditation retreat is writing. Thus, sitting, walking, writing, are all moments of practice. The quietest, deepest sits I've experienced have included writing. The writing helps to empty and settle the mind. We then can sink into a quiet pool, into silence, out of which all of those tumultuous thoughts were created in the first place.

In True Secret retreats, we do timed writings as an equal practice to sitting and slow walking. The bell rings, we sit; another bell rings, we walk; a third bell, the students pull out their pens and notebooks from under their mats and accept their minds as it comes to them on the page. The bell rings again and they read aloud what they have written. Another bell, they do slow walking again.

The classroom is set up as a zendo (a place to sit) with cushions (or chairs) lined along the four walls and an altar in one corner. (You could use chairs in rows if there are a lot of students and, of course, an altar is not necessary.) But whatever the form, "structure" is the modus operandi. If you have a good structure, you make room for the mind to drop deeper, the breath deeper, the writing deeper.

"Anchor your mind with your breath," I repeat to the students. Then, I ask, "And how do we anchor the mind in writing?"

"With pen on paper," they answer. And then, they always ask the question: "What about computers?"

"Even though we can drive, we have to continue to remember how to walk." I answer, "A computer is fine, only it's a different physical activity. A slightly different bent of mind comes out. Not better or worse. Just different."

Handwriting is the first physical way we learned to write. Hand connected to arm, to shoulder, to heart. A computer is a two-handed activity. A different structure. For many people now it is the main writing tool. That's okay, but what if we grow poor and can't afford a computer anymore? Or our electricity gets cut off? This retreat is a training to write and reflect under all circumstances. When we are not always reliant on outside tools, we have a flexibility and freedom.

The meditation retreats of the seventies and eighties did not include writing practice. As many of us sat still, we played out over and over in our minds an upcoming wedding, a lost love, economic worries, raging sexual desire, a recent death. These were true concerns, but we couldn't stop the compulsive repetition of thoughts. Coming back to our breath as a way to return to the present moment was often inadequate and we sat consumed by emotional scenarios of grief, hunger, anger, desire, regret, and resentment. Even though the idea behind sitting is to finally let go of thoughts, to stop burning in hell, often the sitting only aroused and increased our internal aggression, with no relief. A few determined souls managed to rip through their thoughts, but a lot of us continued to boil. Others just checked out and fell asleep on the meditation cushion.

Oddly, I still have great respect for this method. It was a great opening, our first meeting with the ancient monastic life of China and Japan. Though I never attained eternal peace from thoughts (which actually would be a misunderstanding of mind), I learned to sit still (a huge accomplishment in our fast society) and through that to receive and listen deeply, not only to a movie or song but also to hear the trees grow and be enfolded in silence. I learned structure—of a room, of a day, of a week, of time, and of the mind. And I learned about an intimacy in moment-to-moment life, a love I never knew possible and a larger vision of human reality.

The sixties generation, my generation, was willing to drop out of society and live extreme lives until we tore through to some raw truth, some hope of saving ourselves—and all sentient beings. This determined willingness of our generation helped to plant the dharma, the ground of reality, in America. A few rounded a corner, became priests, and made Zen into a career. But many of us spent years on the cushion as lay students until we were finally tossed out into the world, wondering what we'd been doing and what we should do now. Many felt the anxiety and stress of simply figuring out how to earn a living.

Since then the life of practice has changed. People are no longer willing to be so extreme. They demand a more integrative approach that includes work in the world, family life, and the new under-standings in mind science and psychology. Writing practice offers just that. Including writing practice in your daily life cuts through repetitious, obsessive thinking. Writing down those scenarios, pouring out your immediate thoughts on the page, either wipes them out—they're said, done, expressed—or helps you to make sense of them, integrating them into your synapses and muscles.

Right after we write in retreat, we read aloud our pieces with no editing or comments. People are always allowed to take a pass on reading their writing, but as the engine of accepting the mind roars louder, almost no one passes. They feel too much exhilaration in the freedom from the critic or editor, or what I call monkey mind, that mind that jumps around and never lands.

"When we listen to each other read, we are studying mind. Not good or bad," I say. We get to hear the burning, roving thoughts of the people we are sitting with. Reading and listening brings us out of ourselves and we feel relief. We are not crazy. Others have all these wild thoughts, too. Sharing opens compassion and alleviates isolation. *I am not alone.*

In these retreats a person is backed into a larger world. You enter a larger mind as you bend over your notebook. Backed into a connection with all things, a glimpse at love through sorrow, through a glint off a glass or a step on gravel.

I uphold a different form of writing—a priori writing—before novels, short stories, essays, memoir. Writing practice grows strong spines, a confidence in your experience, a belief that your life is valuable (and through that a recognition of all life), an understanding of the mind, a writer's most potent tool, and also an understanding of practice—how one creates. Not only do we do a retreat schedule, but we also sign up for jobs: sweeping the porch, filling water pitchers, ringing bells, lighting candles for the three sessions a day. We ground ourselves in the physical care of our environment.

Did I mention the retreats are in silence? Ten years ago silence was quite a gnarly subject: people were aghast at the idea. Now it's been around and talked about, if not practiced.

I tell the students, "Don't throw it all away with yada yada—talk, talk, talk. Hold your stories in your belly. Pour them onto the page. Later you can talk. Don't diffuse your energy."

Four years ago, at dinner on the first night of a retreat, before we were to go into silence the next day, a student was laying out, scene by scene, a play he planned to write, to three other students sitting around him. I knew he hadn't written a word of it yet. I could tell because if he had he wouldn't have been expounding on it.

I leaned over, fork in hand, and said with a smile, "Matthew, shut up."

He was an old student who'd been coming to Mabel's from New Hampshire for years.

He was startled, then embarrassed, and then laughed.

"They are all going to steal your great idea." I put some lettuce in my mouth.

After students have attended a silent retreat, they say they will never go back to the workshops where students speak the whole time.

In the True Secret Retreats, we are silent during meals and breaks and mornings and evenings. The exception is when we read our writing aloud or have book discussions. I always assign two or three books for the students to read before they arrive for the week, among them *Crossing to Safety,* by Wallace Stegner; *Things Fall Apart,* by Chinua Achebe; *Heat,* by Bill Buford; *The Florist's Daughter,* by Patricia Hampl; *The Spirit Catches You and You Fall Down,* by Anne Fadiman; *Native Speaker,* by Chang-Rae Lee; *Brothers and Keepers,* by John Edgar Wideman. I have them read books because I want our practice of awareness to meet the world.

Literature tells us something real about our lives and reveals an aspect of awake, alive mind. My Zen teacher, Katagiri Roshi, once said, "Literature can tell the truth about life, but it can't tell you what to do about it." Practice roots itself in our actual suffering, in the bones of our writing, expressing our genuine life force. It does not need to be a magic perfect island of formal bowing and Japanese decorum and aesthetics.

When the students read *Walking with the Wind: A Memoir of the Movement,* by John Lewis, I asked them why we'd read it before this retreat.

Nathaniel from Massachusetts responded, "Because Lewis and the other civil rights activists are sitting and walking, like us. They give us an example of how to do it in the world."

◆ ◆ ◆

On one particular August retreat on the last afternoon, we car-pooled, keeping silence (though one car out of the eight sang gospel as they drove), passing sunflowers bobbing their heads along the two-lane highway, passing Herb's Lounge, making a left over the bridge, following a dirt road along the Hondo River where it meets the Rio Grande in the ancient pink-cliffed gorge. We went there to swim, running upstream along the bank, then floating on our backs down with the current.

Some had never been in a live river. Three students had learned to swim, nervously anticipating this trip. They were more reluctant at first in new bathing suits (one is English and called hers a bathing costume).

The day before, it had rained hard, a summer monsoon in late afternoon, and the river was now ice cold. But practice cut through resistance. We didn't think. We dived in.

After days of silent practice we experience each other more deeply. No busy words block our connection in the river. We can feel the new swimmers' glee and pride as they float feetfirst. And we take pleasure in their pleasure. Our minds are soft enough to include the high blue sky, the crisp rippling water, the swallows' nests hanging under a rock ledge, and the cedars along the shore. At this point in the week, practice resonates throughout our bodies and makes room to receive what is around us.

Driving back I thought, *No one else is doing this—so intricately interweaving the practice of sitting and walking with writing, with literature.* Some teachers are now adding a few sessions of writing in meditation retreats but the writing is still considered a separate activity. Not integral to the practice.

I've dedicated my life to this writing practice. Looking back at the long line of cars driving on the crooked dirt road out of the gorge, I realized that I needed to share these retreats—and the next phrase came, "before I die." I feel an urgency. How can I help, knowing impermanence is at my back? What trace of this wild and woolly life—before cell phones, text messaging, fax, iPhones, Facebook—can I leave?

The structure in this book extends the practice from ten-minute timed writings I have taught for years into all the time in which you also live outside the notebook. But that time in the notebook creates an enduring power. To find your writer's voice is to find your spine; it is to connect your breath of inspiration with the world's breath.

Sometimes, I admit, I am hesitant to share: I feel half begrudging—"let them sit long hours like I did"—and half "I am afraid of watering down the teachings," of creating an easy American hit before students move on to something else. But I've found out that that isn't a fair assessment. It has been twenty-five years since my first book, *Writing Down the Bones,* came out and people continue to persevere with writing practice. Frankly, it has surprised and impressed me. Twenty years after the first workshops, students tell me they've had writing groups going all this time.

My job has been to take the ancient teachings and make them relevant. I have not diluted them but put them in an applicable form for our current life by putting writing into the heart of the practice. It's how I can best honor those years in the zendo in Minnesota with my Japanese teacher—and many weeks of practice I did in other lineages from Thailand, Vietnam, and Burma.

Something stays alive because it can adjust, flex with the times. It also stays alive if it touches something elemental, essential in our minds.

Really there is no Zen. I use Zen as an excuse, an angle, a good structure that helps to expose the human heart, that big body of an undefined country. We all have an innate intelligence. How can we uncover it? Believe in it? Care about something as ephemeral as peace and make it our goal? To settle into the bosom of the world and watch dark and light play out—and as my old teacher Katagiri Roshi used to say, "not be tossed away," to record it all on the page.

This book is Zen and not Zen. It is lay Zen; sitting and then stepping out into the suffering of the world—of Auschwitz, the Congo, Native Americans, your friends and family. It is also catching a taste of the joy—and lucky fun—that are possible.

A recent letter from a student summarizes the effect of practicing sitting and walking in order to create a solid foundation for the writing: "Once in a while I remember wading into the cold water, then finally plunging all the way into the Rio Grande, and I am reminded to dive into my notebook and keep going—like with the current—and as in meditation—to get to that space in my writing beyond monkey mind. I know the important part is to keep showing up, not the 'where' I get to. To slow walk, to keep meditation practice. Most of all I am reminded to let go. To let go of self-judgment. All people have something of value to voice." Sit. Walk. Write. That's the true secret.

PART ONE

◆ ◆ ◆

Basic Essentials
The Ground of Being

I beg to urge you everyone:

Life and Death are a Great Matter

Awaken, awaken, awaken

Time passes quickly

Do not waste this precious life

—Evening chant, written on the wooden han

The Greatest Pleasure

Writing is for everyone, like eating and sleeping. Buddha said sleep is the greatest pleasure. We don't often think of sleep like that. It seems so ordinary. But those who have sleepless nights know the deep satisfaction of sleep. The same is true of writing. We think of it as no big deal, we who are lucky to be literate. Slaves were forbidden to learn to read or write. Slave owners were afraid to think of these people as human. To read and to write is to be empowered. No shackle can ultimately hold you.

To write is to continue the human lineage. For my grandfather, coming from Russia at seventeen, it was enough to learn the language. Today, it's our responsibility to further the immigrant dream. To write, to pass on the dream and tell its truth. Get to work. Nothing fancy. Begin with the ordinary. Buddha probably knew, but forgot to mention, that along with sleep, writing can be the greatest pleasure.

Two days ago in mid-August, Santa Fe had a hard rain after months of drought and forest fires. Thunder clashed, lightning flashed, and the heavy dark gray clouds looming over the town finally dropped their glitter all over roofs, trees, arroyos, tomato plants, roads, cars, indiscriminately, beautifully, shining everything up. After standing in the rain in quiet awe, watching the water spill off the roof canals into my two dry compost heaps, I went inside and lay down to feel it drip through the screens and open doors.

Get up. You have things to do, I said to myself.

And I answered, *Leave me alone.*

I kept lying there on my bed, glorying in the shattering sound overhead and then the sudden loamy fragrance that sprang out of the dry grass and filled my bedroom. This mid-August Saturday afternoon would not last forever. It rained so hard I almost thought I was young again, back in summers on Long Island, everything dark and green.

The doorbell rang. I jumped up. A neighbor in a raincoat, small tendrils of wet hair stuck out of the hood, stood in the doorway. Dripping, she came in. I made black tea and took out a chocolate bar from the freezer, opened the wrapper, and lay its cubed belly out on the table.

I hadn't seen her in at least two months. When she had stopped by then, her family was falling apart and she had shared the details. She sensed her husband was having an affair, her thirteen-year-old daughter was smoking dope in the upstairs loft, and the cat was peeing in the corners of the living room. She had wrung her hands and tears ran down her face. She was usually a woman of tranquility.

I listened intently. Who was the husband going out with? Was she sure?

She suspected a colleague: her eyes grew large.

That day two months ago was blistering hot, enough agitation in itself with no misbehaving cat or daughter.

This afternoon, when everything felt new, she nattered on about her roses, three new poems she had written, and how in the last week she was writing nonstop on a novel.

I ventured forward. "And the husband?"

"Who knows what he's up to," she said with a flick of her wrist. "Yesterday he lay on the living room floor for hours listening to music, not moving a muscle."

Doesn't anyone in my neighborhood work? I thought, but asked, "And the affair?"

"Who cares." She shrugged her shoulders.

Her face was relaxed, open; she seemed younger by ten years.

I pushed a little further. "The cat?"

"Oh, Sweetie-Pie. She's taking her pee outdoors."

"The daughter?"

"Would you believe it? She's taken up the violin."

"The dope?" I couldn't help asking.

"I don't know. I haven't worried about it."

As I walked her to the door, I stopped. "I have to ask, what changed your whole attitude?"

"A good question." She stopped and considered. "I'm writing. I'm writing again. Everything is in perspective. I'm back to myself." A big smile whipped across her face. "I have my own life back. Writing feels too good to let other things get in the way."

"You mean it can be that easy?" I asked.

"Of course." I watched her walk down the already drying hard dirt road.

My job has been to spread the writing gospel. I've said it should be part of the Declaration of Independence: ". . . certain unalienable Rights, that among these are Life, Liberty, and the pursuit of Happiness"—and writing.

Sometimes in the idle noodling of my mind, I wonder if I'm deluded, making it all up, how important it is to write. Because writing has fed my life, I've taken the unprecedented leap— everyone needs to write. Like eating a good peach pie and then looking up from your plate and declaring peach pie is the most important thing. But it seems that, when I lag behind in my campaign to get Americans writing, to trust their minds and to know what they think and feel as a basis for democracy—when I only want to dream and wander down summer roads—someone else knocks at my door to inspire me in my pledge.

My friend David Schneider in Germany just emailed me this paragraph from the acknowledgment page of his upcoming book, *Crowded by Beauty: A Biography of Poet and Zen Teacher Philip Whalen* (to be published by University of California Press):

> "You know what's wrong with you?" my teacher began, turning his remarkable attention on me, enclosing us in it, as if we were not sitting in a lively, crowded booth with several other people, in a lively, crowded brewery, in a mid-size town in France on a

warm evening. Such a question leaves the devoted student few options. This information is exactly what you are supposed to want to hear from your teacher, regardless of the emotional color with which your evening, day, week or month will be dyed by hearing it. I made some sort of response—possibly non-verbal— indicating how delighted I would be to know. Not that he was waiting.

"I was thinking about it," he said, looking into my eyes, tightening the focus around us in a way that eliminated any other time and place. "What's wrong with you is that you're not writing. You need to be writing. If you feel you can't do it with everything else that's going on, then I,"—here he used a lengthy version of his name and one of his titles—"am now formally giving you this as a practice to do." Then he released me from his focus, and turned back to the beery merriment of the gathering. He did this without hurry, but somehow abruptly. With finality. There would be no explanation, no commentary. He immersed himself so quickly and thoroughly in other conversations, that it now seemed impossible our "exchange" had even taken place. But I knew it had, from the uneven breathing I felt, and from the mixture of shock and gratitude slowly branching from my heart out to my limbs.

Writing is not just for someone who wants to write the great American novel. Some people know at an early age they want to write; for some it is obvious to everyone else—usually they are mad for reading—but it takes a long time for the understanding to bleed through to them. They don't start till they are thirty, forty, fifty.

Dorothy at eighty-eight had been to five other workshops but couldn't come to the recent December silent retreat because she had hurt her knee and had trouble walking. She doubled her physical therapy and aimed for the August retreat. She and Martha, a woman she met ten years ago in Taos, wrote often together, even though they lived in separate West Coast cities. Martha died recently and Dorothy wanted to make it to Taos again for Martha. She told no one of her plans to come, for fear her daughter wouldn't let her go. She schemed secretly in her eighth-floor apartment where she lives alone, practicing her walking up and down the long hallway, passing the closed doors of other apartments. The day before she left, she found a companion to travel with her and to help. They took a train from Seattle to New Mexico, changing in Sacramento. She put Martha's name on the altar in the zendo and when she read aloud in class she faced Martha's name.

> Martha, I've wanted to tell you how much I enjoyed our first workshop/retreat with you in room one. The retreat writing room was packed. I remember you sitting outside by the chimney mending your leather shoe with a needle and thread. Then I see you slow walking around the same building. I knew you only briefly before we went to Taos. Our trip took us to Santa Fe, off Sunset Blvd and Los Angeles—both places we stayed in hostels. All the details of our trip are secure in my memory.
>
> I remember when you were wheeled into the hospital. I was privileged to accompany you to the intensive care unit. You had only one lung for more than 20 years and it was failing. You couldn't talk. You motioned to your sons for paper. You wanted to write. You and I had written on your dining room table for several years. We would also sit in a quiet corner of a restaurant. Now you were on a ventilator.
>
> There was one more option, to go to a hospital 35 miles away. There they filled your lungs with salt water and then pumped it out, there was a chance that your heart, because of the salt, would continue to beat. You wrote short pieces of poetry but mostly messages to your two adult sons. Your heart continued to beat for more than 16 hours and you never stopped writing. You continued to indicate need for more paper. I asked her sons what were her last words. They said for us to be good boys.
>
> Several weeks later the boys had her memorial celebration.

I was honored to speak. I said that she was my bosom friend, a way of describing a best friend in my era. Then I said how we became bosom friends was through writing together. We followed the practice we learned with Natalie. There are still people who ask me if I will start another writing group. I can't answer that because you, Martha, will not be there. I've been meaning to tell you how much I value you.

Dorothy Sheldon

Dorothy, having made her triumphant journey, felt free to interrupt me in the August class at any moment: "Natalie, do you remember the year someone asked you if you read the Bible? And you answered, 'No I don't. I only read my own books.'"

The class burst out laughing. I turned my head: "I vaguely remember that. Dorothy, I'm afraid you have an extraordinary memory."

She grinned back at me.

Why Silence?

Behind writing, behind words is no words. We need to know about that place. It gives us a larger perspective from which to handle language.

In a silent retreat, our thoughts, memories, and feelings have a chance to come home to us. And then at some point, if we are diligent in our silent practice, our thoughts, feelings, memories, understandings—all of it settles down—and we are where we are—in this very moment. Sounds like a cliché but the floorboards are in front of us, our friend is sitting across from us, the wind and the mourning dove's cry, the hair on our arms, the nose on our face, we are with it all. We do not end at this bag of skin. In silence an unspoken closeness rises up between you and the other people in the room. Someone cries in the corner and you feel it. *Intimate with all things* is a saying in Zen. It is true. Please try it.

If you do not have a group, spend an afternoon not speaking, at the same time still going about your business. At the dentist, nod; at the postman, wave; at the store clerk, smile. You meet an acquaintance in the street, shake hands. You'll be surprised how little anyone will notice you are quiet. Everyone is too busy talking. And if you refine your quiet over time you will carry something much needed in our world. You will carry peace inside you.

Our society is based on talk—talk, talk, talk. But where does this talk come from? It comes out of silence; sound and silence are interconnected.

The silence in which the True Secret retreats are conducted seems extreme in our society. But what is really extreme in our society is talk, nonstop, all the time, to communicate, cover up, divert, share, hide, lie, fill time, waste time, idly, languidly, incessantly. I do not think silence is holy. It's another perspective, a way for our chatty society to stretch.

It's important to know the other half of the coin; otherwise, we are off center, often running away from the intimacy of quiet, the discomfort of just being with another person or with a room of people. Not to mention how much we miss when we are always talking. We forget to receive the environment and to be aware of the person we are talking to.

My friend Katie Arnold and I hike for an hour and a half once a week on one of the trails in the Dale Ball system near my house. We have established a routine: hike up in silence, go down talking. It is such a relief for both of us to have that initial shared accompaniment of quiet: I notice better the switchback where the trail splits, the single ponderosa, the heaviness of my breath on some days, the ease of climbing on others. The trail has become familiar—during snowmelt, in the dark shade of rocks, in early hard spring winds tearing through the last brittle cold crust of a particularly hard winter.

We've noticed that, hiking down, our talk is immediate, close, forthright. We are beaming from the exertion and the direct silent connection with ourselves. Even if the talk is raw—Katie's father, a *National Geographic* photographer, dying of cancer—it radiates, pours over us as we tumble down the trail. I look forward to her recent ventures into cake baking and I pronounce a sudden realization about an author.

The silence is so ingrained now that, for the first half of a hike, I treat it like gospel. Katie and I have become the Vatican. I hike with Seth, Ann, Baksim. I say: we do the first half in silence—and they nod, of course. Isn't it the creed, the constitution, and even better, a relief?

Yes, silence can be an avoidance, a suppression, a way of hiding, a shyness, a secret that never gets examined, a solidification of the lost heart.

In a silent retreat I'm asking not for a rigid taping of our mouths shut while inside we are bursting to speak. Instead, I'm asking to have a relationship with silence, to find that middle ground where we accept and relax into a still place. But, of course, guarding that still place is a lot of noise even if we don't talk. Immediately our thoughts revolt; they have been given free rein for so long. They dominate, want to continue to run the show and express themselves. And we are scared. What will we find inside, if we quiet down? In a silent retreat we are left with ourselves.

Silence has been used as a punishment, *the silent treatment, the cold shoulder.* Or you might have come from a family where no one spoke or one that thinks silence is being impolite. But silence can also be a relief. We don't have to perform or be anyone. Just relax.

In the retreats we do read aloud our own writing and in group sessions we also discuss books we've been assigned. But the background of silence, from wake-up to sleep and through meals, gives us a more thoughtful, digested discussion. And we learn to listen better to each other. It's a slow conversation, not a competition or a monologue. Listen, think, respond. Pretty nice. Then as a group we grow together in our understanding and appreciation of a book.

Ideally, through the practice of silence we become nimble and can roll from talk to repose, not stuck or frozen in either. Silence can be the door to listening, which is one of the great cornerstones to writing—and also to eventual peace and reconciliation within you and in this world.

Meditation (Sitting)

A young girl, Mykala Gillum, comes from Milwaukee every summer for six weeks to visit her grandmothers, both of whom are friends of mine, in Santa Fe. Ten months go by and there she is again. Now she is eleven, just out of fifth grade, and full of jokes they tell each other on the public school playground.

Here's a riddle she related at dinner:

> What has seven letters?
> It is impossible to do?
> If you eat it, it will kill you?

A long pause. None of us could think of the answer.
I threw out for no reason, "A snake."
Mykala shook her head and laughed.
"Okay, so I wasn't brilliant. What's the answer?" I scowled.
"Nothing."
"Nothing." My head snapped around. Kids on the playground behind chain link fences in the Midwest are talking about *nothing*?
"Yeah, you can't *do* nothing and if you eat it you'll starve."
"Pretty good." I smiled.
Then she told another joke.
I didn't hear the first line—I was busy eating—so this is how I heard it:

> A woman goes up to the counter and asks for a cheeseburger and fries.
>
> Ma'am, this is a library.
>
> Oh, excuse me, she whispers, can I have a cheeseburger and fries?

This one really sent me over the edge. It felt so avant-garde, odd, surreal, made no sense. What existential realm of emptiness were these kids grappling with?

Later I found out it was a dumb-blonde joke—kids mirror the deep prejudice of society. I liked my version better—without the beginning explanation. It was much more bizarre, uncontrollable, mysterious, coming out of nowhere, ungraspable. I was excited that some new awareness was making its way unconsciously into the elementary classrooms, but, alas, the next joke she told was about snot (after we'd finished dinner).

But here's the question: that blankness that the mind draws when we try to answer a riddle or understand a joke, can we make friends with that? With not having an answer? With the final root-less inability to grasp anything? Look around. There is nothing that doesn't eventually fade away. We are left with "nothing."

After the big 1989 earthquake in San Francisco, my friend Geneen said, "I always thought I could rely at the very least on the ground below my feet and then the earth was shaking and crack-ing open."

To know this groundless truth and yet not to become desolate, disillusioned, fatalistic. To come right up against the emptiness of the notion of a solid self, a solid existence, a solid thought, and be willing to taste its true transitory nature. There is nothing to hold on to.

That is the goal of sitting practice. Of sitting still. If we can even say such a thing as a "goal" as we sit in the middle of nothing.

But, of course, we all believe there is something: a train to catch on time, an apple to pick in the fall, a coin we dropped by the park-ing meter to retrieve. All of this is true. It is a moment. It cannot be held on to and made forever. Even your wedding will end. It will be a memory only you carry. And someday none of us will carry anything. We will die.

What a terrible introduction this is as a way to encourage you to meditate, to sit still. Please excuse me. But what freedom when you sit down in the middle of your busy life, to unroot the urgency, the feeling that everything is an emergency. To drop down into your breath as if into a luxurious couch, to drop down into the animal bone structure of your body, all at once feel the intimacy with what is around you, breeze through window, bird call, phone ring—your boss wants you working overtime. Even staying close to that. Nothing is that important—and everything matters.

So sit still for five minutes a day. You can do this with legs crossed, butt on round cushion, back straight, eyes closed or open, unfocused, looking down at a 45-degree angle.

Or you can sit in a chair. A good thing to learn: to meditate in a chair no matter how nimble you are and how your legs can twist like a pretzel. Then you can meditate on airplanes, in airports, in the dentist, lawyer, unemployment, Realtor waiting rooms. Take whatever's on your lap off your lap. You can tuck your purse, notebook, laptop, or groceries under the chair. Sit with feet flat, a hip width apart. Back straight. Hands on thighs, palms up or palms down.

Or you can meditate standing up. In line at the druggist—or at the cafeteria in school.

The main thing, whether standing, sitting—even lying down—is to feel your breath go in, filling your lungs, mixing the outside with the inside and then out again—mixing the inside with the outside. We are not alone. We are not separate. Take in life. Give it back. One breath at a time.

So you have a thought, hear a sound, feel an itch on your nose. If you choose the breath as your anchor, then keep coming back to feeling it as your steady staff in this wild and hungry life. It is so easy to be tossed away. To believe everything we think and feel as gospel, to be attended to immediately. If a bomb is dropping, please run for cover; if a bullet is flying, please step out of the way. But if you have a thought of a bomb, acknowledge it and return to the breath. Our suffering is real but it's our attachment to it that compounds it, that creates suffering on suffering.

A student I knew well died. I receive phone calls from other students, who were close with her. "I'm angry. I didn't want her to die. She was my best friend."

I listen. Death comes to all of us. Each situation is different, but it comes. The suffering comes when we don't accept death. The pain is real. We miss our friend. I miss my student. The suffering comes when we fight the naked ache, try to push it away, make it different than it is.

This student is now underground about one hundred miles from where I live.

Well, go dig her up, I think.

Nat, she is dead, I say back to myself.

I argue. I am protesting.

I can do that all I want. But the raw truth is she is gone. When I stay close to that, I am close to my true pain. Our lives are impermanent. I can fabricate, react, defile, spit in the face of it all. And then I come back to the raw fact: death.

This is like meditation. Do you see? My mind, body, emotions go all over the place and when I settle and get to the bottom of things, there is my breath—or in my student's case now: no breath. I find that finally when I distill my overwrought reactions, the truth has few words. *I hurt* or *I miss her* or *no* in the face of what I cannot change.

The same week my student died, my ninety-seven-year-old neighbor died. Even though she was ninety-seven, I did not want her to die. But it made more sense. She was old. But that is our idea of death. We think it should only come to the old. We don't know when our death will come. To understand this is to make our breath more vital. We are alive now. How good to breathe. Come back to it when you meditate and your mind wanders.

◆　◆　◆

I'll tell you a terrible truth: I do not like dogs.

Next door, my closest neighbors have four Chihuahuas. The

mother dog gave birth to three puppies and the couple could not bear to give any away.

They bark early in the morning into late at night. Not every day but they do seem to enjoy their ability to bark.

I decided I could either go crazy with an arsenal of righteous irate indignation or allow it to be. I opted for the latter. (Forget about animal control, police. It doesn't work that way here. I live near Garcia Street and my neighbors all are Garcias.) In winter, doors and windows are closed and the darlings are mostly inside. But come spring they pour out into the yard and the sound pours into my open windows.

Each new spring through late fall I have to remind myself: *Nat, your existence isn't more important.*

But I'm quiet, I argue back. *I do not disturb the peace.*

I have chosen not to control what I can't control. (The two women neighbors are nice enough, offer me fresh trout they've caught when fishing, and they don't think the barking is noise. I hear them cooing to the dogs through the adobe wall.)

When I hear them bark constantly I take a deep breath. *This, too, Nat, this, too.* (I am not an angel—I do run a fan in my bedroom at night to smother the noise.)

My ability to accept the barking has actually given me a lot of pleasure. Oddly, these last four days I have not heard a peep out of them. They are still there but where did they go?

Slow Walking

Driving the two hours to Heron Lake for July Fourth, Mykala, the eleven-year-old grandchild, had another riddle for me: If I'm doing what I'm not doing, what am I doing?

Again, my mind went blank.

But not for long, because Mykala eagerly shouted out the answer: nothing!

Oh, one of those again. I suggested we make up our own riddles where the answer is always *Nothing*.

What does everyone want to lose? Nothing, we screamed.

What costs less than a penny? Nothing, we screeched.

Sometimes to pique our minds I shouted out a topic for the nothing riddle: give me one with gasoline, give me an ethnic one, give me a political one, a Jewish one, an environmental one. I could feel our minds grind and crackle in the car and we threw out anything (that's the way you have to be—willing to fail). Here are some more we came up with as we rolled through the dry hills of Hernandez, past the Abiquiu Dam and the red cliffs of Ghost Ranch:

> What if you have no car and don't need any gas, how much would it cost?
>
> What if Eve didn't eat the apple, what would happen?
>
> Ethnic joke: What happens if you get the *wong* number? (Chinese)
>
> What's worth more than everything?
>
> What did Hitler say about his Jewish ancestry?
>
> What did a drunken driver do when he saw a stop sign?

What did the Indians feel thankful for on Thanksgiving?

What did the man confess when his girlfriend called on his wife's phone?

What's greater than everything?

What do you say in a silent retreat?

What do you want to eat when you've had too much?

This kind of fun has to attend our practice, too. It creates a fresh alertness.

When I do slow walking with students, the basic directions are: Feel the bottoms of your feet as you walk. In sitting we anchor our minds in our breath, in writing we anchor our minds with pen on paper, and with walking we anchor our minds in the bottom of our feet. Feel your right foot lifting, placing. Then your left foot, lifting, placing. Feel how your hips shift, knee bends. You can keep your arms comfortably at your sides or clasp hands in front or back. Eyes focused down in front of you. This is simple, slow. Let the world come home to you. We are always running after things. This is a chance to receive the world.

Then I give the students encouragement: If you don't like slow walking at first, don't worry. I hated it for the first ten years of my practice life. If you have trouble grounding in your feet, take off your shoes and walk on gravel. Slow walking is different from aerobic exercise. What are you accomplishing? Nothing, we scream. There is no particular place you are heading, nowhere to go, nothing to do. Just place one foot after the other.

But sometimes we become somnambulistic, not paying attention, walking like zombies. I call out with no forewarning, okay, now walk backward. Or I command in the middle of slow walking, stand still, arms at sides. Feel your feet, how they hold you up. Are you standing on one foot more than the other? Closer still: as we walk again, notice three new things about your walking that you never noticed before. Have an ancient curiosity. What is this "walking" we do all the time? Notice the moment your foot lands completely on the ground before it pushes off again.

We need ways of paying attention when attention lags. How can we alert ourselves again? We think in our society we have to do something new and exciting—skydiving, car racing, climb to Everest—in order to feel alive and alert. But we can enliven ourselves doing what we do with a little tweak, a little tug. Sit, walk, write—whole universes of liveliness and attention, pleasure are available. Take advantage of this one great life right here and now, even before journeying off to the Bahamas, or Tibet, or Madagascar.

But traveling is a fine thing, too. Bring sitting, walking, writing with you to increase your pleasure of where you are and where you have been.

Here's something else that you might try: driving practice. Drive below the speed limit. And if you are on an empty country road, see how possibly slow your car can go. The first time I did this was in Taos on Morada Lane with Wendy Johnson, a writer and friend. Bob Dylan's *Time Out of Mind* had just come out. We blasted it, rode slow, real slow, maybe ten (maybe fewer) miles an hour, feeling Dylan's gritty voice, his words, the roll of the tires on dirt, the breeze, movement through space, with the windows rolled down.

My father would say, "Ridiculous."

It's good to do ridiculous things. Please, not on a highway.

What Is Writing Practice?

We were taught in meditation to continually cut through our wandering, obsessive thoughts and come back to the breath. I understood the importance of this, how we learn to let go, not cling, not hold on. But I also noticed I had a fascination with those thoughts and they weren't just delusion, unreal, rambling—and they didn't let go so easily. I didn't want to reject them. I was entertained by them. I was curious, surprised. So this is what I think? Only the breath as an object of meditation made for skinny practice. I was ready for the fat, the grease, the unruly. What if I actually followed my thoughts, went out into the tangle, saw where they led, used writing as another way to eventually let go? Writing practice is a perfect complement to meditation practice; the fat and the thin, the precise and the clear with the wild and woolly. When you think about it, how can anything be excluded?

Here's what you do:

1. Keep your hand moving. If you say you will write for ten minutes, twenty, an hour, keep your hand going. Not frantically, clutching the pen. But don't stop. This is your chance to break through to wild mind, to the way you really think, see, and feel, rather than how you think you *should* think, see and feel. This does not mean you have to write orgasmic sex scenes smeared with butter to touch wild mind. You might end up writing about toast, your sore throat, your fingernail. But it will be alive, real.

    Yes, even you who have never left home, never stepped out of your gray suit, even you have wild mind, that vibrating force below your discursive thinking, that true connection. It is natural to human life. Get to work and contact it.

You might write for ten minutes and never land. That's okay. If you accept your mind at whatever level it is as you begin to write, if you don't fight it, it will eventually settle. That's what I learned when I wrote down my thoughts and went out into the notebook.

More rules are listed here but the only one you have to remember is to keep the hand moving. That practice alone will teach you what you need to know. These other rules support the hand moving:

2. Feel free to write the worst junk in America. You have to turn over your mind a lot for the gems to pop out. And really in True Secret Retreats and in writing practice we are not looking for the gems, but a way to meet and accept our whole mind. Writing down the boring, the complaining, the violent, the agitated, obsessive, destructive, mean, shameful, timid, weak thoughts allows us to see them, make friends with those parts of ourselves. They won't then rule us. We won't be running from them, or battling them in meditation—or in our lives. Writing practice asks all parts of us to come forward. And when we get out of the way and stop judging, aren't they all their own peculiar impersonal gems?

3. Be specific. Not car but Cadillac. Not horse but palomino. Not fruit but tangerine.

If you can't remember the name of that tree, don't stop writing, just write *tree*. Later you can figure out: *sycamore*. Just keep going. And do not chastise yourself for not knowing the name. Always have tremendous kindness for yourself. You'll get a lot more writing done.

4. Lose control. Say what you want to say, not what you think you should say.

This is enough to get you chugging across the land of your mind.

How you root something is to continue doing it. In the process you have a relationship with your own mind and in accepting your thoughts, whatever they are, you actually learn to let go of them. This is practice.

Someone asks, "But when does it stop being practice and become the real thing, the championship match?"

You know the answer. Practice is not for something else. Practice is the practice of being here with your life and pen now. Go, across the page—or your computer screen—what are you thinking of? Put your life on the line.

Entry

The Opening Point

We have this life. We live it day by day. It passes quickly. Sometimes not quickly enough—we get *despondent, sullen, downcast.* Those are good words. In those slow moments something might appear—a chance to fall through our blistering fast-paced lives to the other side, where we can turn around and view ourselves, take a curious interest. Underneath everything we long to know ourselves. We wouldn't know it though by the way we act— chugging down another whiskey, not listening to our daughter at breakfast, going sixty in a twenty zone. Reaching to get away; longing to come home.

In writing, in sitting, in slow walking, a flash, a moment appears when we fall through and what we are fighting, running from, struggling with becomes open, luminous—or, even better, not a problem, just what it is.

Look for those small openings.

Last week I led a True Secret December Retreat and was so stressed out I didn't even know I was in that state till I sat still. It was excruciating. Every small task that came to mind was an imperative. I knew my tight thoughts weren't real, but I couldn't shake them and land in the zendo. On the second morning out of the left corner of my eye I heard, *Nat, it's about death.* The entire thought screen dissolved, my muscles relaxed. I was there. Nothing else was that important.

What was that voice? Where did it come from? If you learn to look for an opening, an entry point you are developing, a part of yourself that does not get lost, enmeshed with your thoughts, does not believe them as solid and real. That part can help to find a way out of your confusion.

What did "it's about death" mean? I'm not totally sure. Maybe I no longer had the concern about my parents' deaths—they were gone. I was next in line. Maybe unconsciously I was battling my own death by keeping so busy—or I was trying to fit in everything before I died? Who knows. Human beings are funny animals. All I know is those three words worked.

You can't make this opening happen, but you can feed and fertilize the ground. If you never sit still, it does not even hint to that deeper self in you that you are interested. By practice, by showing up, we are signaling that deep motor, that hum of life, that we are ready: *Help us. Pay attention and lead us out of our confusion.*

That's when writing does writing; sitting does sitting; walking does walking. The veil of boredom, resistance, fear, ambivalence is lifted. Old grouchy Natalie, even happy Natalie, dissolves. There is just the thusness, the honesty of the moment.

This all sounds good, but it takes effort. Also a fascination with something other than our worries, our computers, shoveling the snow on our driveway, which bakery has the better bread, the Dow, how I gained a pound last weekend. We have to cultivate a desire for something other than Cheerios and a good time on Saturday night.

I am on a writing retreat right now in Florida. The ocean is right out the window. Each morning I wake and my first impulse is to jump in my clothes and go out on the beach (luckily, it's too cold in this middle January to go in the ocean; otherwise, nothing could stop me), but I know after many years that at the end of the day, I will feel more satisfied if I attend to the notebook first. Inevitably every single morning the other impulse flashes before me. I am continually challenged to show my resolve.

But I must admit, I do have a counterintelligence seduction technique: Nat, if you go to the couch and write, you can have chocolate and a single Coca-Cola—with ice. I'm there, pen in hand, in a flash. Today is the fifth day and "Nat" is sick of chocolate. My only chance now is to find the entry, the opening, where I can write with concentration so deep even the fizzy sugar water drops away.

But please forget my shenanigans. Settling down, allowing all the electrical animals of our mind to be with us, accepting ourselves is pretty good on its own. Yesterday after writing for several hours I looked up, and out the window a dolphin leaped in the ocean. There! it went again. I just saw one—today—writing this. I felt it was signaling, *Keep going*. Take encouragement from whatever is around you.

What if you are in Cleveland in humid heat or in the dry Valley of the Dead or in constant rain for three months in Seattle? Those very things are supporting you—write about them. Don't envy Florida. Florida has its own problems. The cockroaches are almost the size of a hand and they dash under the bureau when I get out of bed. No place is heaven—and every place is heaven.

As a writer I know I carry all the accumulated moments of my life. How to find an entry, an opening to reveal them. It's not unlike having a conversation at a restaurant. With an old friend you might reminisce; with a business partner, tally up numbers; a child, correct his manners. Where's the opening? The break in routine? Dinner with a man you hardly know. He's a good listener. Suddenly a vein opens up in you. You are telling him about your back porch summer, three years old, the barbecue, the dandelions, the stoop, ants, spiders, and Japanese beetles you caught off the mimosa tree your father loved. You think you love this man. Wait a minute. It's you you love. His listening has given you yourself.

I had a student whose father, now deceased, had illustrated many of the *New Yorker* covers in the seventies. To me that is the height of achievement. I adore the *New Yorker* covers. Whimsical, topical, breezy, silly, sometimes pointed, right in the center of current events. His commercial work supported him and his family, but her father didn't want only to create magazine covers. He wanted to be a serious painter.

You can be doing something wonderful, but something else also calls. I am sixty-three and still haven't found a venue, a form, an entry into writing so many things I want to bring to life again and savor. Those things will die with me. I don't want them to. The race is on, but where do I think I'm going? Headlong into the grave. So no rush. We want to handle the lilacs along the way. We want to find an entry into telling things we carry inside; our complicated love life, eating popcorn in a movie theater, sleet falling at 3 A.M., walking railroad tracks, meeting a girl named Lauchlin Learned at twenty-four in an apartment in San Francisco. She was reading *Moby-Dick* and that solidified our connection though I'd never read it. But what can you say about instances that were important, brief—or long—lovers whose ears you touched, their thighs and bellies, times you walked lonely for weeks and could not tell anyone, a month you were happy for no reason, trips you wanted to take and didn't—India, Tibet, Nepal, Vietnam—and what it feels like never to see those places, what disappointment and betrayal feel like in your eyes, hands, mouth.

No one's going to listen if you start blabbering about it. Just like bringing something up inappropriately at the wrong moment in a conversation, you have to find the right moment. You have to find the entry into what you know inside, the way to bring it out so people will listen.

> *Hey, do you want to hear all my memories when I was a boy?*
> *Not really. As a matter of fact, I just remembered I desperately need*
> *bread. Gotta go.*
> *But I thought you were wheat intolerant?*
> *Not anymore and you skedaddle out of there.*

Let's try it differently. "I was thinking how Willie Mays—you know him, don't you?—affected my childhood, ages eight to around twelve."

How so?

Do you see, there is an angle, an edge of curiosity, a nudge.

Make a list of the things you want included in your writing. What angle can you approach them with? What authority can you muster to decide that toast yesterday, burnt or not, matters?

But I also want to say, you may never get the opportunity to write exactly that. Like the man who illustrated the *New Yorker* covers. He never got to the fine art painting, but I bet his life was richer for the yearning and it informed his illustrations.

It seems sometimes I can sit every day and have no opening at all in my meditation. But I am so much richer for having sat. The world opened to me anyway. Just not the way I thought. It did not fulfill my idea, but maybe it fulfilled my life. Think of that. Pretty exquisite.

A Moment

Can you tell me a moment that was big for you, an instant that you saw things differently from then on? Not a sensational moment—you won ten thousand dollars in the lottery, you were lost in the woods alone with no food—but a quiet moment when your whole awareness shifted?

If you are like me, you haven't had very many. But the ones I have had, I've followed fiercely. One was that moment I saw I was going to dedicate my life to connecting writing with the study of mind. I was twenty-three years old and had no idea where it would lead. It's hard sometimes to stay true to it—and yet I am grateful.

I asked a group at Upaya Zen Center to tell me a moment that was big for them. A man in the room, Michael Swanberg, came up to me afterward and told me this: He had been a nurse in the Peace Corps in Burkina Faso (Upper Volta). Only the boys go to school there. The young girls' job is to go in the mornings to the well and collect water for their families. Each day Michael stood at the well with a chalkboard in hand and wrote one letter of the alphabet. That was about all the girls could learn in the time they had waiting in line for their turn at the well. On the eighteenth day after he presented *R*, Miriam, who was ten, had enough letters to spell her name. He was present the moment Miriam for the first time held his tablet and wrote her name, M-I-R-I-A-M. He saw a light go on in her eyes that would never be extinguished. All of a sudden these random symbols meant something. She was the first, because many of the girls had names, Bintou or Zenabou, whose letters were further down the alphabet and they had to wait to complete theirs.

As Michael spoke, I imagined the breath of Miriam's name coalescing into printed letters, the synapses connecting in her mind, thoughts taking a new shape, the dimension of language expanding, cloud and sun and treetop no longer so far away, through fingertips a new extension of communication.

But Michael wanted to tell me something else about that moment with Miriam, because it was also his moment. "I was a nurse and I'd thought I'd start a clinic, but in that moment I understood what education can accomplish, and that education came before health care as a fundamental building block. I started a school in that village for girls."

"And after you left the village?" I asked.

"I went home and got a master's in education at Columbia and now I teach at the University of Virginia. I found my true career."

Years ago my friend Barbara Schmitz told me that at nineteen, naïve and innocent, walking down the aisle to be married, in a sudden instant the church was flooded with light and she knew, yes, this was right. At nineteen, what do we know? We take a chance. (Maybe always in love we take a chance.) But her intuition in that moment held, even though Bob is a wild character, wakes her up at 3 A.M. to watch TV. At Christmas in their small Nebraska town, he hangs flashing lights high over the empty lot next door that read, "May All Beings Be Well and Happy," next to a big neon heart with wings, which makes his neighbors crazy. He's mixed a Sufism symbol with a line from the loving-kindness sutra in Buddhism. What's he talking about? they ask. What religion is this? They scratch their heads. She's had a happy marriage for almost fifty years.

Tony Bennett, the great crooner, has reported that, many years ago, he was involved with drugs. At the time, he talked to Jack Rollins, who was then Woody Allen's manager. Rollins had known Lenny Bruce and told Bennett, "He sinned against his talent." Hearing that single sentence changed Bennett's life: he quit drugs and was set on a whole different path.

It's important to trust these moments and let them inform our lives. Often we have an opening—clear and quiet—and then we negate it. "Oh, that's silly. Oh, I can't do that. I can't live that way." Why not? These moments are a flash, an insight when we see through the confusion of our constant thinking to something clear. How wonderful. Why wouldn't we listen instead of abiding by our discursive, wandering thoughts—I should go to the store, I should buy a car, I ought to check out the new movies, I need a new bathing suit, I look fat, I have no friends, etc., etc.—and follow these thoughts as though they were the holy truth?

On the other hand, we love to mythologize heightened moments, telling over and over the story of what happened. Then we make them outside ourselves and do not take responsibility for what has been given to us. Don't do that. We can be courageous enough, intelligent enough, capable enough to take these insights on and let them inform our lives.

Right now, survey your life. Make a list of those moments. What did you do with each one? Which ones did you ignore? Can you make good on them now?

Happiness

I have been sick for the last three and a half weeks. I can write "flu" and be done with it, but that is a generalization.

My eyes were bloodred—the doctor said it was conjunctivitis. Isn't that what little kids get? I asked. My eyes were caked shut in the morning.

Some lump was developing in the bottom of my mouth. I coughed up green phlegm. My ears were ringing and I heard things as though I were underwater.

Shall I go on? Why do I feel the need to state all this? In the middle of these three weeks I read *The Makioka Sisters* by Junichiro Tanizaki and the book was long and slow, magnificent and included everything. Many details about the main characters' colds, allergies, bug bites, intestinal problems. And as I read, I didn't cringe or back away. We are in human bodies and sickness is natural, part of this physical life.

I must admit by the time I got to 530, that last page, I did take extra delight in the final line. The third sister was finally going to be married—one of the strong narrative drives throughout the book— and the result: "Yukiko's diarrhea persisted through the twenty-sixth, and was a problem on the train to Tokyo." And so the book ends.

We are left with the ginger hesitation of a woman in her thirties— late for marriage in mid-twentieth-century Japan—riding to her destiny, the body engaged and nervously pumping. Now don't be a prude. You have to love it. The honesty alone. No one else tells us these things. Thank the writer for being honest.

While I was sick, I also lay in bed and read *Freedom* by Jonathan Franzen, *Unbroken* by Laura Hillenbrand, *The Tortilla Curtain* by

T. C. Boyle. I'm not a fast reader. Three weeks, full-time in bed, is a long time. Occasionally I'd look up through my bedroom window and watch slow, dry spring sketch in pale green to the distant willows and near lilacs. And sometimes I'd pause to sneeze, cough, blow my nose, take a sip of tea.

Friends would call to commiserate. Yes, I was awfully sick. It did seem a long time to be in bed—then I'd return to the dream of the book in hand.

The truth is I was happy. Happier than I'd been in a long, long time. And I knew that as soon as my energy returned I'd plunge back into mad activity, full of passion. I was lucky that I loved most of what I did. But as I lay in bed, I realized passion was different from happiness. You don't *do* happiness. You receive it. It's like a water table under the earth. Available to everyone but we can only tap it, have it run up through us, with our stillness. A well that darted around could never draw water.

We misinterpret success, desire, enterprise, even things we love, as the state of happiness. Mostly in my daily life I don't even consider happiness, so busy dashing after life, defending, building, developing, even fighting, asserting, arguing. I'm in the scramble—lively, engaged. Our society emphasizes power, dominance, the individual. We find intensity and industry in war. Otherwise, why would we keep engaging in it, if we confessed its reality of misery, fruitlessness, and destruction?

Where does happiness come in? That give-and-take, that meeting of inside and outside. Isn't that what reading a good book is about? Even enlightenment is a meeting, a relationship of the inside and outside. You don't wake up in a vacuum. Buddha glanced up and saw the morning star and with that sight his whole nervous system switched gears. You can't be at home with yourself in a cubicle. To be at home with yourself is to be at home in the world, in the interaction with others—and trees, slices of cheese, the broad, sad evolving of politics.

Peace is in happiness. Our society rarely considers peace, the harmonious interaction between human beings, their environment, and the working out of conflict in a way that is not harmful, that always has the sights on fellowship, care, the cessation of hostility. We call it a breathing spell. A time to feel the in and out of our breath, to be simply human. Buddha has said peace is the highest good. I think we all agree he wasn't a dope and yet nowhere do I see true peace valued.

When I was sick, I was settled down. I didn't have a lot of energy for engagement, the daily tending to a hundred details. I am not saying the ideal state is a sick body, but I noticed last night as I began to aggravate about something that I knew I was getting better. When the bite of concern, worry snapped in, I was reentering the pale of human life. At that moment, where was my happiness? I lost my connection to home plate, to the core of reception, patience, the bottom of my belly, to the ground of well-being.

The next day I dragged myself out of bed, and went in the next room and crossed my legs, sat up straight to sit for a half an hour with the idea to anchor my wandering mind in the breath. To keep coming back to the present moment. To regain the contentment I so quickly lost.

I often tell my students, "Don't give up on what's here. The love you want is no other place."

As I sat, I was lost for a long time in a memory of Auschwitz, where I meditated for five days last summer, then in the thought of turning over the compost out back in my yard, then considering maybe buying some granola. Thoughts have no hierarchy. The mind jumps from the serious to the mundane in a second. Then, snap. I came back to myself. If I want happiness I have to understand it and then dedicate myself to it moment by moment. I can't stay in bed sick all the time to attain it. I have to commit myself to it when I'm also well.

The thing I love about the Zen koans, those terse, enigmatic teachings from the Chinese ancestors, is that they include sickness in their presentations to realize original nature.

> Great Master Ma was not well. The director of the monastery stopped in his room and inquired, "How is your health? How are you feeling?"
>
> The Great Master replied, "Sun Face Buddha, Moon Face Buddha."

We could speculate on meaning here but the important thing right now is that sickness is included in the realm of realizing peace, understanding, and happiness. Nothing left out.

How to stay connected to contentment in the dentist's chair? To be with peace as I listen to the news? Sometimes happiness is being in the center of our grief.

When my friend's husband died in his thirties and she was bereft, her therapist said, "Enjoy your grief. You'll miss it when it's gone." Can you imagine that? To be in the heart of your life whatever your heart holds.

I am not saying there is a prescription for happiness. Just that the trained mind examines situations, does not simply fall apart: if you are sick in bed, it's an opportunity. If you continually have a hard time with a friend, look deeper than the bickering and misunderstandings. Maybe the relationship died years ago and you neglected to notice it and hung on to old ideas of love. Maybe it will take root again—maybe not.

In college, the single class that caught my interest was an ethics class in the philosophy department. We studied Descartes, Bergson, James, Kant, Socrates, the full gamut of dead white Western men. The essence of each reading was the question of happiness. What is it? How to attain it?

When I studied with my Japanese Zen teacher, he said, "Whatever you do, let it be accompanied by dharma joy." He lifted his dark eyebrows in an expression of inclusion. Yes, you, too, Natalie, are capable of this. At the time I was thirty-one years old.

No one can hand over happiness on a silver plate—or on a doily.

Especially when we don't know what it is. Our job is to pay attention and examine it. Can we have happiness, peace at the same time as joy, fun, pleasure, anger, aggression? How do we learn to abide in ourselves?

Amazingly, I ended up staying in bed for two more weeks. Five weeks in all. That's a long time. My ears, the eustachian tubes, became congested. Little blood flows there. The middle of my head was filled up.

Finally, on a Wednesday, I had some energy and went out. Eagerly I plunged into life again. How foolish I was. I must have done thirty different tasks, including going out that night with friends. I enjoyed it all, but just as I was falling asleep, I asked the question, *Were you happy?*

Quickly the answer came: only the half hour I was planting tomatoes and strawberries in the backyard.

The next morning I woke with that long-faced stranger, loneliness, sitting beside me. Certainly I've been lonely before but this time it glowered beside me. I'd lost paradise, that long time I had in bed.

In the next days at different intervals I asked, *Are you happy?* Head deep in my active life, I didn't know how to find it again. I couldn't make it happen. Then just seven days out of bed, standing in line at the bank, like a cocker spaniel or possum, I felt happiness, for absolutely no reason, ringing my bell. After I made my deposit, I sat in the car and asked, *What happened? What did I do?* I was almost "bursting with happiness" as they say in romance novels but I was not particularly in love, only swimming in my own being.

Then this morning as I dressed to go out, darkly blue, from allergies and constant May winds and a drought that made my skin almost crackle, I asked myself, *Are you happy?* Checking in, a reminder of my new search. And I growled, *No,* but I wasn't convincing. Some defense had been smashed. Even in misery there could be happiness. And then it bubbled up, clear and full, for no reason.

But there was a reason: I was paying attention. Happiness had been waiting for me all these years. The Declaration of Independence declares our right to it, but we forget to pursue it. But you can't really pursue it; it arises and with our attention we notice it. Instead we end up stampeding over it, buying things, or creating great suffering through hate, prejudice, frozen ideas.

Happiness is shy. It wants to know you want it. Like pursuing writing. You write the truth. It signals more truth to rise to the surface. You can't be greedy. You can't be numb—or ignorant. The bashful girl of happiness needs your kind attention. Then she'll come forward. And you won't have to be sick to find her.

Some Determination

Because the True Secret Retreats are in silence, I have a bowl next to my sitting cushion where students leave questions and comments. Often they don't sign them, but deposit anonymous thoughts folded up on small square pieces of paper.

Sometimes I come a few minutes early to the zendo and rummage through them. Sometimes a specific comment gives me the trigger for a talk or a writing topic.

On a Tuesday in August I unfolded a square and burst out laughing. In pencil was written: NEVER MIND. Can you see the whole action of thoughts in that moment? The urge forward, the grappling, then the letting go. I saved that little piece of paper in my wallet. The whole world in two words.

And this afternoon another square of paper fell out of my notebook from a retreat five months ago: How do I/does one keep from turning an intention to practice into a "to-do list" and then into "I should"?

That's a good question, don't you think? We do that all the time. We want to meditate; we want to write, run, quit drugs. The list is endless and it becomes a fight. I want it; I don't want it. I am ashamed, disappointed I didn't do it. It was a dumb idea. I didn't really want it or I didn't think I could do it anyway.

But that's not true. Some seed, some hunger, longing, was real, was awakened below our discursive, shifting thought patterns. We water that seed with our effort but then the effort gets misguided. It becomes like my student's question, another thing I have to do. We've lost the deep connection.

So how do we stay connected? First we admit in our heart of hearts it's something we sincerely want. And then we move toward it. Sometimes we fail for a week, a month, a year, a decade. And then we come back, circle the fire. Our lives are not linear. We get lost, then we get found. Patience is important, and a large tolerance for our mistakes. We don't become anything overnight.

I have a close friend, who for a long time was a deep Zen practitioner. Even if no one else showed up, she sat alone day after day in the zendo. This went on for ten, fifteen years. Then it turned on her. She couldn't go near the zendo or the sitting cushion. She had burned herself out.

For ten years the thought of meditating made her sick.

This month she moved to a new house. I went over to visit. She had a whole room set up as the altar room.

"Hmm, might you sit again?" I asked.

A little smile crossed her face. "Just a little bit. In the evening before I go to sleep."

Were those ten years she didn't sit part of the practice? Was she composting a new approach to making sitting alive again for her? Maybe, because there was still heat—she disliked it so much. She was still connected, disturbed. Energy was alive. Not comfortable, but below the surface something was working.

When you use drugs, alcohol—anything that numbs your consternation, your grappling—then you can really get lost, cut off from your true desire. But in the struggle, in the "shoulds," "the list," there is an indication, a direction. You want something.

Sometimes we show up with no heat or heart. Our practice is dead. Better to go down the block and have a thick shake or an apple.

Bernie Glassman, on his fifty-fifth birthday, threw a birthday party for himself for five days on the steps of the Capitol in Washington, D.C. Those five days were some of the coldest in D.C. history. Wrapped in a blanket and coat, he sat each entire day with one question: "What can I do about homelessness, AIDS, and violence in this country?" He'd been practicing Zen for many years, but he still had no answer for these pressing problems in our society. Sometimes when he sat, fifteen people joined him, sometimes more. Together he and his friends pondered the question. When the five days were up, he had his answer. He was going to establish the Zen Peacemakers Order.

This is a beautiful story and a good example of direct determination that does not get sideswiped with the wandering mind or forgetting what you are about.

The key is to be "engaged." Pick something that matters to you—something you continually show up for has a chance. And even when you lose your way, you can come back. The returning over and over builds the spine of practice. Can you have the heart for that? Be patient.

Otherwise, your life will be like a water bug, always skating on the surface. You don't want that. Not in your secret real core. You want you. Practice is a way to meet you.

What Is Practice?

I use the word *practice* all the time. Students nod, but after some time it became clear that different definitions were at work.

On the first day of a yearlong intensive, where we meet for one week of silent retreat each season, I asked students to choose a feasible practice that they could do for the whole year. At the end of the week they read their choices aloud: to stop eating fries and lose twenty-five pounds; run five miles a day and strengthen their quads; do an hour of sitting, then an hour of writing, then finish their novel. The lists went on like this. Full of achievement, forward-looking, industrious.

I felt like a lightweight when my turn came: to sit for twenty minutes five days a week.

Right then I could have had a discussion about practice, but I decided to see what would happen.

We met again three months later, in spring. The first night right after dinner, I asked, "So how did it go?"

Some smirks, head shaking. "Not so good? Well, you know, you can change it for next time," I said. "Let's go over what practice is."

Why didn't I save them from unrealistic ideals or workouts in the first place? Because I knew they wouldn't listen to me—oh, they'd listen, after all they were my darling students—but they wouldn't hear me. Struggling with something, failing has a great effect—a gap opens, you realize you don't know everything—a little emptiness forms where you can receive something. Particularly in our Western ambitious, productive, drill, workout society it is hard to hear what's at our backs; we only pay attention to what's in front, advancing, a goal. Not succeeding brings us to the ground, to look outside our shell, to even use the small word we are afraid to use: *help.*

So in that meeting in early April, the spring wind howling out-side, and the tiniest bit of pale green edging cottonwood branches, we established a different slant to practice other than "practice makes perfect": It's something you choose to do on a regular basis with no vision of an outcome; the aim is not improvement, not get-ting somewhere. You do it because you do it. You show up whether you want to or not. Of course, at the beginning it's something that you have chosen, that you wanted, but a week, a month in, you often meet resistance. Even if you love it, inertia, obstacles arise: *I can make better use of my time, I'm tired, I'm hungry, this is stupid, I need to listen to the evening news.* Here's where you have an opportunity to meet your own mind, to examine what it does, its ploys and shenan-igans. That's ultimately what practice is: arriving at the front—and back door—of yourself. You set up to do something consistently over a long period of time—and simply watch what happens with no idea of good or bad, gain or loss. No applause—and no criticism.

"That's why," I told the students, "you should take a bit of time in settling on the practice you want to do, because it needs to be a con-tinuous commitment. It needs to be realistic, something possible."

I chose sitting five days a week, because I knew I needed flex-ibility. Some days of the week I would miss. It's good if you can do it in the same place and time each day, but with modern life it's not always possible. So I kept my commitment simple: twenty minutes five times a week. If I already had missed two days for the week and it was Sunday, the last day of the week, at 11 P.M. and I was tired, I sat my twenty minutes anyway. I sat it tired, maybe even nodding off a bit, but I did it.

But why? Wouldn't it be better to just go to sleep?

No, this continual practice expresses your true determination, signals to your unconscious, to your deep resistance that you mean business. (And then your resistance roars louder and you roar back.) Over time, this practice kicks in that strong motor, that deep imper-sonal life force within you. It reinforces and supports your yes to life for no reason—not because you were good or bad or worthy or kind or successful, but because, like a blade of grass or thunder or a cloud, you are alive.

Last year someone gave me a peony that sat in a glass of water on my kitchen table. It kept opening. I'd walk in at any time of the day or evening and it was screaming gorgeous for no one, no reason, except it was doing what it was alive to do.

Practice awakens that force in us. But not without being challenged, and we have to do it in spite of logic, the quirks in our mind, our heavy opposition. What practice builds in us is a true confidence that can't be derived from outward signs of success—fame, money, beauty. This confidence comes from the fact that you show up over and over again. That you do what you say you are going to do. That you commit to a practice, one that is possible given your life and maybe with a few missed times, a few times you mess up, you stay in the driver's seat. And even the times you don't show up are part of the practice if you pay attention to them, do not get rigid, can develop a soft heart/mind and don't punish yourself or quit altogether because of one—or two—times you didn't sit, or run, or write, or eat perfectly.

Isn't that what happens to people who diet? We blow it with one meal and quit altogether. That's because a diet is goal-oriented. We have to lose those twenty-five pounds or else. We punch our bellies; we fight ourselves. We are here and want to be over there. We hate who we are to begin with. Not a good idea. Hate only leads to more hate.

How can we make a diet into a practice instead? Maybe decide to eat healthy? Too vague. To eat vegetables at least three times a day? To eliminate sweets? To promise to drink eight glasses of water five days a week? I don't know the exact answer for you. Sometimes we back into losing weight. The result of another practice: awareness.

At the end of the last intensive, titled "Deep and Slow: The Path of Practice," on that final afternoon when we broke silence, we went around the room, sharing our experience of the year.

A small smile spread across Brenda's face. "Did you notice I lost thirty pounds?"

No, we shook our heads.

Wasn't her practice writing every day? I thought.

"Well, I did. The silence was new for me and the quiet. The nonrushing, all that time—I had time to notice things. On the second morning back in winter at breakfast I said to myself, *Brenda, you don't have to eat like there is no tomorrow. There will be lunch. There will be dinner. You can relax.*

"Then I looked around and saw what the skinny people had on their plates. Let me tell you they didn't have as much as me. I kept watching the skinny ones and how they ate—and then I imitated them. I guess that was my real practice this year."

What if you choose a practice and you're not sure it's your way? a student in the new intensive asked.

You won't know, will you, unless you try?

These new intensive students at our spring week reenvisioned, more realistically, what they were going to do. On the outside, some of their practices sounded bland, not heroic, not conquering, but let me tell you, inside our crazy minds, to cut through discursive thoughts and resistance and show up is valiant, lion-hearted, staunch, dauntless.

I asked them to keep a notebook, a record of their practice. I showed them mine of the last three months: a small, light journal someone had given me a long time ago, bound by staples, made from banana fiber, peach-colored.

I open it now:

> March 5th—skipped. (First day I wanted to begin, right off didn't do it)
>
> March 6th—7:30 a.m.–7:50
>
> March 7th—7:25–7:45 a.m. at Mountain Cloud by myself
>
> March 8th—6:25–6:55. I sat a half hour. Always relief
>
> March 9th—Friday, sat in Palo Alto by creek

March 10th—sat outside Mill Valley library. Sat again for 20 min. with Wendy facing ocean in Sausalito

March 11th—sat with Bill Addison & Michele on ground, Golden Gate Park—big fog

March 12th—skipped, traveled home to N.M.

March 13th—sat in morn.

March 14th—terrible menopause, lay down rather than sit up, 2:30–2:50

March 15th—sat in morning, house studio, moved to deep place, feeling B. J. Rolfzen from Hibbing

March 16th—lying down practice, wiped out

What I see looking back is that I even pulled my friends into the practice. I didn't write an evaluation of the sits—no good or bad. I did them even when I traveled. And even if I didn't feel well—I meditated lying down. The practice was lively. I didn't think, *I am an old-time meditator—why am I doing this light practice?* I had my container: five days a week, twenty minutes. I had my recording notebook. Off I went.

The notebook helped to keep the relationship with my practice going. I see:

April 2nd—skipped, went to Ghost Ranch with Joan Halifax*

---

*I thought I'd address this right here to help with any confusion: Two women Zen teachers, both named Joan, their last names Halifax and Sutherland, live in Santa Fe, both on the same street across from me. I mention both in this book. Halifax is the Abbott of Upaya Zen Center and Sutherland is the Roshi (teacher) at Awakened Life, where she conducts a weekly koan salon I often attend. Santa Fe is not a large town, population about sixty thousand, yet Joan seems to be a powerful moniker here. The poet laureate of Santa Fe is Joan Logghe and another Zen teacher in Albuquerque, sixty miles south, is named Joan Rieck.

Sometimes it gets confusing. Once Joan Sutherland was visiting, sitting in my living room, when a friend popped over. I introduced them, only using first names. The three of us chatted for forty-five minutes.

A day later my friend called and said, "I never imagined Joan Halifax to look like that."

"You're right, she doesn't. That was Joan Sutherland."

Joan had walking pneumonia and I dragged her over boulders, repeating: it's an easy hike. Clearly a torrent had ripped through this arroyo recently and lifted whole trees by the roots. And the storm clouds were gathering over our heads. "We have to find an escape route onto higher land," she repeated. "Oh, just come further. It's one of my favorite hikes." Another crack overhead and she shot up the straight wall of a ravine. (Even with pneumonia that girl could move.)

April 3rd—sat at 5 A.M., rained through the night

April 4th—skipped

April 5th—skipped

April 6th—skipped

Even though I skipped—legitimately or not—recording kept a continual relationship. It wasn't a blank, a shaming, just a note, "skipped." I stayed in connection.

Practice cuts through our habit-driven compulsions. Where do we think we are going anyway? Through practice we can arrive at a steady still place, even while another part of us—and all society— screams ACHIEVE.

Actually, we are achieving, if this will make you happy. You are achieving an understanding of practice, something that will settle your life, make it real, build a good foundation. Not well-being, but the *ground of being*. That's a large place to have in your back pocket. Pretty good.

After our practice discussion, Beth chose to write a haiku a day for the remaining nine months. A month into it, her son was deployed to Iraq. She was heartsick and worried. But can you imagine, for a small period each day she had to drop everything, open, notice, and find a haiku. A breath in the middle of agony.

Look at these:

Following the storm
a monarch sips a raindrop
from a maple leaf

Mindfulness breakdown:
arguing with my mother
who has dementia

Heart cracking open
with scent of October rose:
mother's favorite

Fitful sleepless night
uninvited visitor
new year comes with wind

THE THINGS THEY CARRIED
reading Vietnam
outside cold grey pouring rain
inside dark despair

Vowing not to kill
I carry an ant outside
on a newspaper

no one else to blame
in my lifetime many wars
not stopped even one

rowing with mother
two loons dive to mud bottom
we skim the surface

only with dumb luck
do we survive our parents
to get on with our life

Young doe on lakeshore
nibbles tender water plants—
I was never wild

1–20–2009
Tuesday, like others
and totally different
Inauguration

Oh, impermanence!
pink magnolia blossoms
scattered on green grass

Beth became a peace activist over that year. She sent me haikus, sometimes one or two on a postcard, especially when she was visiting her mother in Cable, in northern Wisconsin,. She didn't evaluate them, only tried to capture the moment—around her and in her mind.

Recently she was an assistant at a yoga and writing workshop I taught for mostly new students. One afternoon they wrote and then partnered up and read aloud to each other. I walked around listening and happened to pass Beth when it was her turn to read. I paused. I hadn't heard her timed writings in a long time. When she studied with me, her timed writings had tended to stay on the surface. Now I heard deep expression; her words had weight and their own integrity.

When the class gathered again, I turned to Beth. "Do you mind if I ask a question?" I said in front of everyone. (My returning students have to put up with a lot from me. I'm kinder with new students. But maybe not. Let's get down to business. We don't have forever.)

"Beth, I just heard your writing. What happened? In past years your writing practice never quite connected." I leaned a little forward. "Is it okay I say this?" Then I plunged on, "But you're solid now."

She took my question seriously, didn't balk. She understood it was deep curiosity, not criticism—and she was used to me. "I used to try to please the teacher, get my fellow students to like me. Finally I just started writing about the hard stuff in my life and what hurt."

I nodded. The new students were profoundly moved. All week I'd been drumming into them, "In order to write, you have to be willing to be disturbed."

The fact that you purchased a nice purse, have an adorable puppy, had a neat childhood isn't quite the fodder for writing, doesn't have enough grinding energy. But even as I say this, if you can get past the cuteness and touch honest intimacy and true detail, there's nothing you can't write about.

But for most of us, under our polite façades we have roiling, screaming inconsistencies and crazy hearts—let it roll.

Sharyn wasn't sure what her practice should be. She was a longtime student and could write every day or sit, but she wanted something fresh. I don't think it was that she was tired of sitting or writing. They had become second nature to her. She would probably fit them in no matter what. Like brushing your teeth. You don't have much opinion about it. You just do it. And it's good. Voilà, clean teeth. Voilà a few pages written. Voici sitting for a half hour, a check-in with impatience, restlessness, calm—all that energy yours now. Not too much disturbance. Hopefully, you have widened your capacity for acceptance, putting your arms around the whole lot of being human—aggression, boredom, desire in a thousand forms.

Sharyn also did a singing practice over the years. She had a beautiful voice and the song she wrote about learning to waltz became our class anthem.

THE WALLFLOWER WALTZ

Nodding my head, tapping my toe,
I hold down a spot on Wallflower Row.
I learned to walk such a long time ago—
Teach me to waltz.

Sometimes I'm shy. Sometimes I'm slow.
I fall out of step. I step on your toe.
I'm wanting to waltz more than you know—
Teach me to waltz.

Teach me to walk on air—
You know I'm halfway there.
Dance with me if you dare:
Teach me to waltz.

Teach me to waltz real slow.
Teach me to just let go.
Teach me the things you know.
Teach me to waltz.

When I am gray and eighty-two,
Regretting the things I never did do.
I'll be able to say I went dancing with you:
Teach me to waltz.

Put down your fiddle. Put down your bow.
I am still here on Wallflower Row:
We'll make it sweet. We'll take it slow.
Teach me to waltz.
Teach me to waltz.

Sometimes when we are doing walking meditation around the zendo, one slow step after the other, anchoring our minds in the bottoms of our feet, I ask, "Does anyone have a song?" Someone begins to sing, "Hard Times Come Again No More" or "We Shall Overcome" (by a woman who was part of the Freedom Fighters in Mississippi)—everyone has some song important to them. And while they sing we continue to put one foot after the other.

After a hard day of wrestling with our minds and hearts in deep silence, we all realize we are in some way wallflowers, shy, broken, closer, and truer to the human condition. We feel relief when the room is filled with Sharyn's voice actually articulating our human-ness. We can relax, accept, and fall deeper into ourselves. And then we find inspiration. What do I want to do if I last till "eighty-two"?

As she was looking for a "fresh" practice, Sharyn was also in a new painful situation at home. After she had been working many years as a recreation leader in an inclusion program for kids with disabilities (autism, Down syndrome, deafness), because of bud-get cuts her hours were reduced from five days a week to one, two, three, or four days a week. Every week was different and they didn't inform her of her schedule till she arrived at the beginning of each week. Obviously this was maddening and disrespectful. It felt as though they were purposefully creating these obstacles as a way to edge her out. Hopefully she would quit. She was the highest-paid employee, with a lot of seniority.

During that April week of the intensive she wrote about the pain and instability of each week facing that job. She was also dedicated, committed to the kids who came over the years, and she did not want to abandon them. Repeatedly in her writing she vowed, I will not quit. They will have to fire me.

At the same time she was surprised to find herself writing about happy childhood memories of summers when the family spent time at Lake Shasta.

> One of the greatest gifts of my childhood was the swimming we did on our family vacations. We would drive up to Lake Shasta twice a summer and camp on a rocky beach for four or five days.

There I could swim in fresh water and hot sun, blue sky above me and water everywhere. Before I could swim I mud-crawled, suited up in an orange, over-the-head life jacket, a bathing suit and a pair of Sun-Glo sandals to protect my feet from the rocks. I crawled along the edge of the lake, half-in, half-out of the water.

I had formal swimming lessons at El Cerrito Pool after I was too old to mud-crawl and I did fine floating with my face in the water, floating on my back, but it was those vacations at Shasta that formed the foundation of my happiness. From the time the sun rose high enough in the sky to warm the water there was nothing to do but swim, play in the water, float around on old boat cushions or air mattresses, take a turn at rope-tending or skiing behind the boat. We had to be called in from the water to eat lunches of melted peanut butter on stale bread. We had to be restrained from going back in immediately. We had to be forced to put on T-shirts over our burned skins and to sit still to have Sea and Ski rubbed into our shoulders and backs. The T-shirts clung and wrinkled in the water, making cold and clammy pockets, robbing us of the feeling of warm sun on our skins.

The second week ended. I would not see the intensive group again till late summer.

To my great surprise Sharyn came bounding into the first meeting in mid-August radiant with vitality, clearly happy and whole.

"Did you quit your job?" I dumbly asked.

"Nope, it's still the same. But I have a new practice. I swim at the Berkeley Marina in a cove below the Shorebird Nature Center. I'm swimming in brackish water."

"What's brackish?" I was amazed at how content she was.

"Salt water from the ocean mixed with fresh water carried by rivers into the bay. As I swim I see the cars going by on the nearby freeway, but also butterflies, seagulls, ducks. I even saw a deer once. I stash my backpack at the Nature Center and leave my towel on a rock and my shoes next to it."

I was mesmerized. "How do you get there?" I knew she didn't drive.

"I take two buses, which takes about fifty minutes, swim for twenty-three minutes, change clothes in the public restroom, and take a ten-minute bus to work. I wear my swimsuit under my clothes and bring a change of underwear and a work shirt. I usually wade into the water to waist height and start out with a front crawl."

Sharyn didn't try to make a practice of accepting her miserable work situation, breathe compassion in her heart to the new director— all our tired ideas of what we think practice is. Instead she remembered something she loved: swimming at Lake Shasta. And she went with that. She didn't try to correct an uncorrectable situation. She built the practice on pleasure—and deep effort. That's a lot of bus riding alone before work.

You don't know where practice will lead. The *New York Times* had an article back in 2009 about a woman, Nina Sankovitch, who pledged to read a book every day for a year and review them on her blog. She followed some rules that gave structure to her practice and kept it going: the more specific, the better. All the books she read, she couldn't have read before. She read a single book per author. And by necessity she mostly stuck to books of 250–300 pages—or fewer.

Besides the pleasure—she said not one day felt like a chore—she hoped maybe to inspire reading in others, but she especially chose to do this as a way through a period of sorrow and soul-searching after the death of her sister.

The article said she had less than three weeks to go. She might not read a whole book for a while once the year is up, but can you imagine a practice like that? It has to change you. Nina was a former environmental lawyer, who now wears a locket with an image of a man on the toilet reading a book.

A regular practice is radical. It is not a habit that you get comfortable with, that you don't even notice you do. The simplest practice if you commit to it regularly challenges you, cuts through. Even if you choose something of deep pleasure, when you give it structure it changes the game.

After long practice, how to keep it fresh? Make a small change. You can sit thirty minutes instead of twenty, four times instead of five times a week. Sit in different places.

The wonderful thing about long practice is the experience it builds; you can sit deeper in your seat. The hard thing about it is you can show up but that's about it. No inner effort anymore. Nothing alive.

I once positioned Miriam Sagan, a poet, as the relationship guru in front of one of my retreats, titled "Doodling Hearts." Someone asked her, what about long-term relationships when you know everything and are bored?

That's your first mistake, she said. You think you know that other person. Well, you don't. And then we think we own them and we put them in a box. And then we say nothing's happening. Pay closer attention. Practice. We don't own or know anybody. Don't let your first surprise be that they walk out the door.

When a Zen friend two nights ago heard I was writing a chapter on "practice," she immediately asked, "You mean sitting and walking practice?"

No, I said. That isn't the practice for everyone.

Twelve-step programs can give a strong foundation. You speak your heart/mind, then you listen. No cross-talking or commenting. Someone signs up to make coffee, someone else collects donations. In a natural way you learn structure. You can't use your meetings politically and you have anonymity.

An opportunity for practice that surprised me is at St. John's College, the Great Books school, in Annapolis, Maryland, and here in Santa Fe. They now have a master's in Eastern studies and I challenged Krishnan Venkatesh, the head of the graduate program, "So you read Asian texts? But there's no sitting, no practice. What's the good of it?"

"The practice is listening to everyone. Sitting in seminar and allowing everyone their thoughts and opinions. Even when their ideas infuriate you."

Impressed, I tried it at the next community seminar I attended, which was not on an Eastern book, but *King Lear.*

At first I almost pounced on the woman across from me and the man cattycorner to her. Both said things I didn't agree with and I was passionate about *Lear,* heated up by my memories of being twenty-three, taking a whole summer seminar on *Lear,* carrying those opinions all these forty years. I didn't want anyone messing with my beliefs. I was a stick of dynamite. In this moment of heat, Krishnan's comment sliced through: "The practice is to allow each person their thoughts."

I took a tremendous step backward and a deep breath. I then listened to the young man, eighteen, who was homeschooled, then the environmentalist lawyer, and the woman with the heavy Russian accent. At St. John's we address people as Mr. Burnett or Ms. Goldberg. And we have our names on the table on cardboard cards. This is to allow some distance. Our comments aren't personal, created to enrage anyone.

I left that seminar feeling luminous. *Lear* had so many more dimensions than I had realized. To allow someone else's mind is to be newly open to our own mind. To abide a whole room of individual thoughts is to feel large, containing worlds, abundant and whole. No enemies. No one to fight. This ability to listen seems a strong foundation for democracy.

So what practice would you like to try? Be realistic. Climbing a mountain a day might not be possible. Be specific: how often, where, when? You might try to find a friend, someone to join you in doing a practice. At first that support is helpful. It could even be someone long distance. You check in with each other on the phone or email. And keep a notebook about your effort. Keep it simple. And don't forget to record the days you skipped the practice. Get your arms around the doing and the not-doing. It's all you—and not you.

◆ ◆ ◆

True Secret
Retreat Essentials

Calling all you hungry hearts,
Everywhere through endless time!
You who wander, you who thirst—
I offer you this Writer's Mind.

Calling all you hungry spirits,
All the lost and left behind.
You who hunger, you who thirst,
Your joy and sorrow now are mine.

—slightly altered verse from Gate of Sweet Nectar

Setting Up

IN PART TWO I want to give you the nitty-gritty of a formal True Secret Retreat. All my practice with Katagiri Roshi in the zendo had to do with attention to detail, the physicality of actually doing one thing after another, taking it in with the body: bow, sit, stand, clean cushion, walk, chant, eat soup in the first bowl, salad with chopsticks in the middle bowl, a pickle in the third bowl. Clean bowls with hot water, drink the water (nothing goes to waste), wrap bowls in napkin and put away.

A True Secret Retreat is not as formal but there are some basic things I want you to know. Maybe translate these instructions into how to help your daughter with her homework—or more ephemeral, how to fall in love.

In any case, I give them in this section so you can better form your life of practice.

When I was young, going to many retreats, my father asked, "But, Nat, when do you advance?"

I smiled—or frowned. Probably laughed. He had a point.

But I kept doing retreat after retreat, moving into wholeness.

But always remember as you learn this specific practice, that it is not only for us. It is also beyond us—to stretch and extend us in service to the world.

Altar

When I was a young girl, the Carosellas lived next door. All the children and the parents were named after saints. Teresa, Frances, John, Vincent, Anne. Every evening they opened the doors to their linen closet, where, instead of towels, sheets, washcloths, there were round glass holders for candles placed on lace doilies, a vase of plastic red roses, rosary beads hung from a statue of Jesus. They said their night prayers together. The word *sacred* was used. "This is our sacred time together." Every ordinary night in all four seasons they sliced out twenty minutes for a hallowed ceremony in front of an altar.

At the Mabel Dodge Luhan House we transform the classroom into a zendo, a place of meditation practice, with black cushions and chairs lined along the walls. Behind where I sit is a kiva fireplace with several rounded shelves that we designate our altar. One shelf is dedicated to the names of the dead we place there and want to remember. Another shelf is for the names of people we most consider our muses, whom we write for, and another is for people who need healing, special care, and love.

Each week that I teach I place on the altar a photo of Shiki, the great Haiku writer, an invalid, who dragged himself to the edge of the tatami mat, overlooking his garden, where he sat all day waiting to receive a haiku. For Shiki the act of creating entailed alert stillness. His awareness gave birth to haiku, to the alive moment when the earth falls into place. Often so subtle you don't know what hit you. Look at this one he wrote:

BEFORE THE GARDEN

Cockscombs . . .
must be 14,
or 15

What does this haiku mean? Maybe he couldn't get close enough to count the exact number of cockscombs—or maybe it means caring enough to care about a cockscomb in the first place? And to accept the mind as not perfect—fourteen or fifteen of them, not exactly sure. This kind of simple attention shifts reality, enough so that Shiki is called the father of modern haiku. Without his "sketch from life" principle, observing what is, haiku might have died out. His attention in the garden kept haiku alive, even though he died of spinal tuberculosis at the age of thirty-five. Much can be done by doing little—with regard. This I want to remember and I want my students to acknowledge the fierce heart of Shiki.

Clark Strand, who wrote *Seeds from a Birch Tree,* gave me that Shiki photo when I had him visit class years ago. He wrote a haiku for each student. I still know one of those students. She treasures her haiku. She is a knitter, and her son, the week before, had been sent to prison. Strand wrote for her:

The wall disappears
and time becomes a sweater
I give to my son

I also place on the altar a photo of Allen Ginsberg in a yellow wood frame, sitting in a white shirt, cross-legged, his face captured in an uncanny smile. He is our muse of raw honesty for the week. An essay of his written in 1974 is titled "Polishing the Mind" and connects the study of the mind with poetry. When I read it, I knew I had found my writing path. I wanted to document and structure a practice for others to follow, a way through writing to wake up. I consider Allen Ginsberg the grandfather of the writing practice lineage.

Sometimes I bring a photo of my grandmother, whom I adored. She was no high being but she was my being. I encourage students to bring photos that are important to them. Probably too many dogs are propped up on the altar. I tell them writing is human to human. But they have their arguments—and I back down. Feathers, bones, stones, small green hard pears in August and plums in late spring also appear.

A teacher friend Ron Makha many years ago built a small table for me out of wood scraps. We taught together in the Taos hippie school Da Nahazli in the mid-seventies. Pema Chödrön, who was Deirdre then, and is now a famous Tibetan Buddhist teacher, taught there, too. I use that table as an homage to Ron and to that time and as the base for an altar I keep at home. It has a photo on it of the old couple, now dead, who were my landlords in Santa Fe for six years, Louise Taichert and Sandy Feldman. Louise was the first woman in New Mexico to receive a medical degree and was also state tennis champion when she was seventeen. Also a photo of my mother just before she died; a photo of my father, studying one of the portraits I did of him; a wooden Jewish star I painted blue that was on the plain pine coffin that Katagiri Roshi, my Zen teacher, was cremated in; a stone pipe from Pipestone, Minnesota. A photo of Thich Nhat Hanh standing next to Katagiri Roshi, both looking small and lost, like two Asian refugees in a strange country, in front of a large elm in the back of the Minnesota Zen Center. A hunk of turquoise I found at an old adobe I rented when I was writing *Writing Down the Bones*; a small silver bowl with a single pearl inside, sent to me out of the blue by Barbara Moran, an old student, referring to the image I kept using at that time in class, "grease your minds, like a pearl rolling in a silver bowl, don't get stuck, caught as you write." A round burn mark is on the wood table from a time

I lit a candle in a tin can and then forgot about it. Luckily, the table did not catch on fire. Also on the altar, placed on top of each other, are three rakusus in their cloth cases, ceremonial Zen garments that I received over the years, one directly from Katagiri when I took lay vows in 1980 on March 1, exactly ten years from the day that he died.

To be honest, for a long time I had a small altar but didn't pay much attention to it. But as though by osmosis it grew in me as I unconsciously passed it on my way to other things. So you might try having one. Do it for your children, for their first poem, first tooth. My friend Ann Filemyr, who studied in the Native American tradition in northern Michigan, has altars everywhere you turn in her house, even behind the toilet. Bright feathers and dried flowers and Indian corn and shells. I don't know if it so much has to do with what she studied, as it is an expression of her being a wild, exuberant woman in love with the world.

An altar for the dead, for harvest, for winter, for birth, for graduating from high school, for the divorce of your parents, for marriage, for a love of horses, for your first kiss, for trees, for the end of war. You can fill the whole house with praise, with remembering, honoring, accepting, forgiving. No room anymore? We have to go live outside in nature, its own great altar.

Schedule

Structure is so important. It's how we learn to order our lives— and order our mind and our writing. If I have all day to write, often I never get to it, or finally only by four do I settle down. Rarely do I have a whole day, but if I look at my calendar I can block in writing time: *Tuesday I'm free from five to six in the early evening.* Write it down and for that hour, do it. You don't argue if you see on your calendar a doctor's appointment. You go. You might even jot down where you will write—kitchen table, backyard, Kakawa Chocolate House—so you give yourself little wiggle room. Then show up.

The idea of structure is to eventually learn to internalize it, so that you can make the most of your day, not to adhere to it rigidly. To learn to balance activity and a time to rest, to receive. Constant doing creates burnout with no space even to know what you want to write—or say. Learn structure early on—it will help to create a capacity even to include pleasure. This is your life; don't blow it. You can't get it back.

We want to help with our country's poverty, suffering, and injustice. At the same time be connected with our family and friends. And how about other countries, the planet's well being—how can we assist? It can all become overwhelming. Structure gives clarity. Clears abstract ideas. Allows us to touch the ground of being. Teaches how to go forth and not become scattered.

A full- or part-time job helps to create structure. Instead of fighting the job, learn to use it for your advantage. Wake early to practice. Several of my students do timed writings or slow walks during their lunch breaks. A built-in structure can be very helpful. Use the weariness after work to write. You are already broken down; no energy for resistance; you can immediately drop to a deeper level.

The True Secret Retreat schedule can be used with ten people, two, even one person. When I first practiced in the early seventies I laid out a day schedule and followed it by myself. (At that time it was straight sitting, no writing. What a delight it would have been to include pen and paper, but it was wonderful anyway.)

Notice the schedule begins rather late in the morning for a retreat. I've found people are often so tired, they can't think straight. Not thinking straight can be good—you break open—but deep rest also opens a person.

An optional reading group is scheduled for the afternoon. This reading group is a cornerstone of writing practice, an opportunity to sit with a group and practice reading aloud with no one commenting. It is asked that you only read aloud something you wrote during the week—not your three-hundred-page manuscript you've been working on for the last five years. The idea is to hear your own naked, unedited voice in the present and to learn to accept it, to stand behind it and not be looking, as we normally do, for praise or criticism. I don't think it ever becomes comfortable to read aloud, but that's what is good—the practice is alive. If it feels naked, you are not hiding and covering up. Writing comes from your true life, not from being polite, cautious, censored. I have done writing practice for thirty-five years and it still feels exposing to read aloud. When it doesn't anymore, I'll be dead.

Usually the person who signed up for reading group for that day on the jobs list leads the group. All that leader does is to set the tone, choosing the readers—everyone who wants a turn gets one—and then a pause, and the next person reads. If you are late in coming, wait outside till the person reading has finished. Once you come in, stay for all the remaining time. You can also come to the reading group just to listen. Usually those people are new and are building the courage to read aloud. It is also fine if a person all week never reads aloud: even in class, they are allowed to pass.

And, naturally, we stress anonymity. We listen in order to study mind and how mind moves. We all have the same principles of mind, we just use different details. No good or bad. We don't listen to pick up gossip on someone. The more our minds accept whatever is read, the more we also accept our own voice and enlarge an acceptance of the world's voice.

It is in these groups that bonding occurs. You hear people's suffering, their predicaments, and compassion is engendered. I don't think there is a group I have taught where at least one person hasn't lost a child, been raped, been betrayed by a spouse, lost all their money, had a fire burn their house, had alcoholic parents. Hearing someone else's tribulations encourages you to read yours, too. A solidarity forms. You don't feel alone. On the first night you might project a perfect life on someone or decide the whole group is just too straight, middle class, too proper, and then over the week you hear their writing and everything changes. In one retreat when we broke silence an African-American woman pulled me aside: "Man, do white people suffer." She shook her head in amazement.

The True Secret Retreat usually begins Monday night and ends at lunch on Saturday. Though the structure has been altered, the experience is based on Zen's ancient roots, something that has worked for a long time and can be relied on. This schedule can be modified for a weekend or a single day, even half a day. The flexibility allows students a way to transfer their understanding to their daily life. I give it here in full because it is helpful to understand its basic bones before you create your own format.

True Secret Retreat
Sit, Walk, Write

MONDAY

6:00–7:00	Dinner
7:15	Meeting in zendo

DAILY SCHEDULE

7:30–8:00	Sit (optional)
8:00–9:00	Breakfast
9:00–9:30	Break
9:30–12:00	Sit, Walk, Write
12:00–1:00	Lunch
1:00–3:45	Break (free to nap, walk, sit, write individually)
3:45–4:30	Reading group (optional)
4:30–6:00	Sit, Walk, Write
6:00–7:00	Dinner
7:00–7:30	Break
7:30–9:00	Sit, Walk, Write

THURSDAY

Lunch–8:00 P.M.	Free (A chance for mindful window-shopping, writing in café, etc.)
5:00–6:00 P.M.	Reading group
8:00–9:00 P.M.	(Back in zendo—Sit for an hour)

FRIDAY

Regular schedule

Film in the evening

SATURDAY

7:30–8:00	Sit (optional)
8:00–9:00	Breakfast
9:15–11:00	Sit, Walk, Write
11:00	Lunch

Coordinating the retreats with the seasons is a traditional thing to do. If it is the August retreat, on Friday afternoon we go to the Rio Grande and float silently down the current; if it is the December retreat sometimes on Friday afternoon I arrange for us to go to the Sugar Nymphs Bistro in Penasco, about a forty-minute drive away, where we fill the café, order dessert, and all silently write for an hour. The owner of the bistro is a Zen priest and understands—she doesn't expect us to talk. The drive is beautiful, so we practice "just looking" as the cars (we make a carpool) buzz along. Sometimes it snows in the mountains—an extra treat.

On Thursday, students even have a chance for shopping. I ask students to take three breaths before they decide to buy anything and if they venture out (town is in walking distance), to please maintain silence. "Don't squander the energy you've been building."

The second page of the schedule has simple notes:

Some Notes

1. Silence will begin upon waking Tuesday morning.

2. Please be on time at beginning of morning, afternoon, and evening sessions. Step in and out of the zendo with your right foot.

3. Bowl by altar is to leave notes with questions, etc.

4. Bring Jamaica Kincaid Tuesday morning, Jimmy Santiago Baca to Wednesday afternoon, Willa Cather to Thursday morning, Binyavanga Wainaina to Friday morning. Beforehand, note parts you want to read aloud.

5. Silence will be broken before dinner but after Shabbat service at around 6:30 on Friday. Silence will resume upon waking up on Saturday through 11:00 when we are finished in the zendo.

6. Please take off shoes before entering zendo.

7. Yoga can be done in the log cabin.

Being on time is respectful. Stepping in and out of the zendo with your right foot is a moment of mindfulness. You rush to get there on time; now you are here, stop a moment, step in with your right foot.

Number four of the note page refers to the names of authors whose books were assigned to be read ahead of time. I ask students to mark parts they like as they read. Those parts can be shared in the group when we come together. We go over the books in class, beginning with naming the physical structure of each book, to come to recognize how the author built his or her story.

In number five Shabbat is a short Jewish service of lighting candles, drinking grape juice (the retreats are alcohol-free), and sharing pieces of challah (braided egg bread) to usher in a time of peace and let go of any of the problems of the week. It's a sweet way of ending the silence and brings in a Western tradition. I learned it many years ago from Rabbi Zalman Schachter when I lived at the Lama Foundation and found that non-Jews also love to celebrate Shabbat. I am Jewish but was brought up nonreligious. How do I resolve the differences between Zen and Judaism? I don't. I'm both a Zen practitioner and a Jew. They enrich each other. I become more of who I am. My students don't have to change their religion or heritage to participate. They become more vibrantly who they are. "The moon does not get wet when reflected in the water nor is the water broken or disturbed by the moon's reflection" (Dogen).

Orientation

First Day (Sitting), Bowing, Job List, Meals, Interviews

Don't be reverent when you sit. Be alive—inside and out, to yourself and what's around you. Meditating is not an opportunity to be holy or to zone out, but to wake up even if it's to awaken to the ache of the world—or your knee or a sniffle—what do they feel like? A memory arises—where did it come from?—where is it going? And who is thinking? Get to work. No slacking.

1. First Day (Sitting)

At the most recent winter True Secret Retreat I asked the students on the first day during afternoon break to sit outside for five minutes, do slow walking outside for fifteen minutes, and stand still outside arms at side for one full minute. It was mid-December and nineteen degrees. The reason I asked how they did with these assignments before we began the afternoon session with a half-hour sit was not the cold—though one student sat facing the cemetery at Kit Carson Park, using a timer because she was afraid otherwise her face would freeze or she'd cheat and run—but to enliven the room before the sitting session. Even with the sharp chill, I could feel a dull dutifulness this first afternoon, yes, sit, yes, walk, but we'll do it more like zombies. It is true many arrived the evening before and were still jet-lagged or stunned by the dry cold or big sky, but this simple sharing reminded them of their own presence, revitalized their energy, so when the bell rang three times for the thirty minutes of sitting we were more alert, more settled, more present whether our shoulders hurt or we were remembering our father's recent death or feeling the breath was a wild pony never to be caught.

2. Bowing

On this first day when the schedule still feels strange and new, bowing is another awkward action.

"When we bow hands together in front of us at the end of sitting or walking it is not mandatory, especially if it is against your religion," (no one laughs at my little joke—they are very nervous and new).

The bowing is a silent, formal way to acknowledge ourselves and the people we are sitting with in the room.

"If it doesn't feel right, please don't do it."

3. Job List

That first evening they also sign up for jobs:

Lighting Candles

Snuffing Candles

Filling Water Pitchers

Sweeping Zendo

Sweeping Porch

Leading Silent Reading Group

Ringing Bells for the 7:30 A.M. sit

Town Crier

The Town Crier is a position we recently devised. At the end of each session the student states: "As a reminder please keep the silence for yourself and everyone." It seems to hit home. It works.

I tell students, "It does not matter if the floor looks clean and you don't think you have to do it. If it's your time to sweep, sweep. Forget about the evaluating mind." I pause. "If we evaluated, we'd never write a word. Sweep your mind clean. It's a pleasure to shut up and just do something."

It's a delight to ground yourself in the material world. I used to sign up eagerly for cleaning toilets in the old days of Zen and scrub like mad with that bristle brush. Just recently I was assigned bathroom duty every day on a ten-day silent retreat. While sponging the sink, disinfecting doorknobs, replacing toilet paper rolls I lost the sense of time. There was no me with my angst. Only the luminosity of the white porcelain bowl, the feel of the mop handle, the visual squares of the floor tiles.

We have no bathroom duties on True Secret Retreats. What my students are missing.

4. Meals

The old saying "We are what we eat" fails to catch we are *how* we eat. I know a Buddhist teacher who studied for a long time at a small monastery in Southeast Asia. They had one meal a day—you can imagine how hungry he was when mealtime came around. His teacher told him that the first three bites should be chewed fifty times. You can picture the dilemma—hunger versus mindful attention; how to modulate your most primal drives? Each student had an interview with the teacher every day and the first thing the teacher asked was, How many chews?

I do not ask this of the True Secret students—but maybe I ought to. Instead we place a simple meal service on the windowsill in the dining room. Students may or may not pick it up, take it to their seat, and read it silently before eating their meal. It acts as a reminder to pause, to feel gratitude, and to remember how extensive, far-reaching this food before us is.

SIMPLE MEAL SERVICE

1. *We remember this:*
   We have food while some have none
   We have each other while some are alone

2. *Food Offering:*
   All you demons and hungry ghosts
   Whose desire is never satisfied
   Share it with us
   Be at peace

3. *Out of the mysterious source*
   We and the things that sustain us come.
   Waking and eating, embracing and sleeping,
   We walk on the empty sky

4. *We are grateful for this food—*
   The work of many hands
   And the sharing of other lives

The Food Offering is traditionally done at lunch. I tell students to place a small piece of lettuce, a chickpea, a lentil on the edge of their plate and after lunch they can place it under a tree or in the garden. "Please no grilled cheese sandwiches, a quiche, a whole pickle, a spinach pie, a cookie," I tease them. We all carry inside us hungry ghosts and demons. We include them here with this simple gesture and hopefully allay their suffering.

Numbers one and three were taken from Joan Sutherland's *Open Source Sutra Book*. So many of us have times of feeling secluded or lonely or simply singular. Here it is honored, included. And the third entry feels poetic—of course, poetry should be at the meal. "We walk on the empty sky." A big embrace of the "mysterious source," not nailing it to one image as though we know for sure where it all comes from. We each meet our provenance in the act of practice—or when we trip out the door trying to evade it.

Food and eating is a tricky balance. How to enjoy it and not cling to it, how to eat enough, not too much, how to nourish and then let go.

No exact prescription works. You have to find your own way in this great expanse.

5. Interviews

Every second afternoon of the retreat a sign-up is posted for interviews, four students at a time. Each group meets with me for roughly twenty minutes that evening. We sit for a few minutes to settle, then each student tells how the week is going and if there is a question. Twenty minutes might not seem long enough, but it actually cuts right down to the bone—no time for dillydallying.

A designated student for the evening leads the group of four in slow walking back and forth from the zendo to the interview meeting in a log cabin, about a city block's distance away from the zendo. If I linger with one group, the group waiting slow walks in a circle outside.

Meanwhile, everyone who is not waiting for interviews or who is not in the room with me is practicing in the zendo.

I ring a loud resounding cowbell I found in Nebraska years ago to alert the new group to enter.

The value of a small group meeting rather than individual one-on-one meetings with the teacher is that it breaks the hierarchy, is more relaxed, and, most important, the students have an opportunity to hear and learn from each other's hearts and minds. It alleviates the teacher-centric structure and, in truth, it is easier on everyone.

Dreams and Lying Down

Mabel Dodge was an heiress who had an artists' salon in New York and visited Taos in 1917. When she went to Taos Pueblo at the foot of Taos Mountain, the first man she saw there came up to her and said, "I know you." She looked at him and realized she'd dreamed about him back east. He was Tony Lujan, who became her husband and was the first pueblo Indian to marry outside the tribe. She became Mabel Dodge Luhan (with an *h* so people wouldn't mispronounce her name). Together they built the Mabel Dodge Luhan House at the edge of pueblo land. Georgia O'Keeffe, Ansel Adams, Paul and Rebecca Strand, Willa Cather, Carl Jung, Jean Toomer, John Marin, Marsden Hartley, Robinson Jeffers, Frank Waters, Mary Austin, and others were guests at the House. Mabel wanted these people to experience the life of the Indians. She felt America was going to hell and these artists could communicate to the public a new way to live. The windows on the roof bathroom were painted by D. H. Lawrence. There were no curtains and he wanted privacy. The man who wrote about sex turned out to be a prude. Mabel traded a ranch she had in San Cristobal, seventeen miles north of Taos, for the original manuscript of *Sons and Lovers*. Lawrence's ashes are interred at this ranch now run by the University of New Mexico.

Mabel's dream of Tony cut across time and space and eventually created a whole new environment that almost a hundred years later is a place we use for retreats.

1. Dreams

On retreat we don't only have the luxury of looking at a romantic dream like Mabel's: we have the opportunity to face hard, grotesque, telling dreams that come night after night, including to me. I'll turn to the students on the second or third morning of the week and ask, "So how many of you had tangled dreams last night?" I raise my hand and two-thirds—or maybe half—raise their hands. Other hands going up is a comfort. *I am not alone,* lost in my own loony world. (You might be, but now you have company.)

Why do we dream like this during retreat?

In the silence, the paying attention through sitting, walking, and writing signals our unconscious and tells it, *she's listening.* So the wild mind of our natural universe throws out all kinds of hooks, maimed and screaming characters—it's their chance to be heard. So listen to them. It's an opportunity to drop limited vision of time, space, and being. What does it mean to climb up an ice wall to find a man at top with a needle in his arm and a bag of green cabbage roses on his head? I don't know—and maybe you will never understand the exact symbolism. But the whole scene is calling to you to be included.

At the very least, write down the dream. As you write, see if any associations come up. If they do, follow and explore them. Then let them go, not as in getting rid of them, throwing them in the trash. But let them recede into the background and be another thing that supports you on your way.

I just sat a ten-day silent retreat where I was not the teacher. I was surprised how little my sitting practice was ruffled, no great obsessions; if anything enticing came along in my mind, it didn't have much grip—*Oh,* I noticed, *you again,* and the thought faded, deflated. But at night I dreaded going to sleep. In the morning the bedsheets were mangled. And I woke for long hours in the middle of the night staring. I had one dream of a brutal decapitation, another about missing three deadlines in one week and destroying my life, and in a third it was the day before my birthday and no one was wishing me Happy Birthday.

The first three days I tried to ignore what was happening—I was so enjoying my daytime tranquility. But finally I had to face the night. How? I had to include it. When I woke I grabbed my notebook and wrote down the dreams. This was a retreat that discouraged writing. Most meditation retreats do, thinking it's an escape, an indulgence in creativity—instead they ask sitters to bring it all into your sitting and walking, to face it there and let it go. And I am a goody-two-shoes, so in my life of formal practice, even though I include and believe in writing when I lead a retreat, I try to obey the edict of other teachers. But in breaking that structure on this retreat I came back to my own authority and to knowing what I needed to do for myself. I did it quietly, not flaunting it, not disturbing the basic structure. But it helped me settle into a deeper wholeness, including the demons, the electric animals of the night. After that I felt a fuller presence when I sat—and a friendliness. All those pals from the dark forest were sitting with me. A whole army of unacceptable characters. What more could I ask? It opened the boundaries of my mind. No limit.

2. Lying Down

It's good to know how to meditate lying down. Sometimes we are sick, have a bad back, so many contingencies come up, but if we include this position we will always have an opportunity to practice. For most of us, unless we have a violent death, lying down is the position we will be in when we let go of this life. I'd like to think we can learn to practice right till the end. Will you go out on the in or out breath? It is said it's the out breath with a rattle sound. But will that be your experience? Pay attention and let us know.

At the True Secret Retreats, we place enough mats at the back of the zendo that three or four people can lie down during the sitting meditation periods. Usually teachers are afraid that, if you let students lie down for meditation, you will lose them—they will fall asleep and snore. But in the twelve years of making lying down available at our retreats, this has not happened. Students have been very judicious in choosing that position. Sometimes they are curious and sometimes they might be exhausted and need a break in structure. Isn't it good to learn to practice and work with exhaustion? A lot of people in our society are exhausted. We drive ourselves too much, worry, anticipate, aggravate. How can we lie down and work with that, feel our breath, in all situations? Perhaps you do nod off for a moment. It refreshes. When lying down is set up as a structure for practice, it does not disintegrate into a pajama party or a "sleepover." It becomes a form for exploring tension, fatigue, the terminal position, not a time to surrender into torpor.

Breaking Silence

If you think silence is hard, you will find that the breaking of it at the end of a retreat is even harder. But there is also the breaking of silence *during* the retreat: sometimes we need to call home to check on children or sick or slowly dying parents. Keep it simple, if you can. Being on retreat is a vastly different place than being in your usual life. When you make that call you are slicing into a busy world and it will come back at you through the airwaves.

Try to stop or keep to necessity any whispering and note-passing to each other. Make a real effort to settle into the silence. But don't be the third person, who sees the note-passing or whispering going on, who condemns anyone who breaks silence. I've spent many hours in my young practice roiling with judgments. Let it go. Concentrate on your own peace, then no one can disturb it.

At the end of a retreat the transition into speaking can be a challenge. It's then I remember a line in the loving kindness sutra or prayer:* *May we have the ease of well-being,* which is about transition. An *ease,* a connection to ourselves from moment to moment, whatever ups and downs, ins and outs or change may occur. Not being jolted by impermanence. We cannot stay in the studio painting or writing forever—or even work; we can't do it for twenty-four hours a day. We have to stop, take a city bus, go home, and greet our family, our partner, our children, our empty apartment.

* *May I be happy*
  May I be peaceful
  May I be free
  May I have the ease of well-being
  May I be safe
  May I be healthy

Once we enter a silent retreat we can't be there forever, either. The days pass and, before you know it, it is the last day. And we face another transition though all along there have been transitions— from sitting to walking, then to writing, to lunch in the dining room, to bed, to wake up, to the changes in our mood, thoughts, feelings. Now there is the one from silence to speaking. We know each other well though no one has spoken to each other. When we are silent and practice together, another level of communication opens up. And we have written and then read aloud. We feel each other more deeply.

At the end of a retreat with my Japanese teacher, no discussion or mollycoddling happened. We sat and were silent; the bell rang at the last sit: we bowed. The teacher walked out of the zendo without a word and climbed the stairs to his apartment; the students walked down the stairs to the basement, put on shoes and coats, and poured out onto the street.

At the beginning I had no idea how to contain all the energy that built up in me during the week. So at the end I went crazy. I'd talk and talk—to my husband, my friends—my jaw was out of control. I had this new wonderful thing: speech. If it were summer, I'd ride my bike down the empty, tree-lined midwestern streets late at night, or in winter I'd clomp over in my snow boots to Häagen-Dazs, sit on the windowsill, spooning coffee ice cream with hot fudge poured over it into my mouth, and look out on the frozen or rain-filled streets. What a glory it all was. Did not everyone stop and notice?

My final direct teaching from Katagiri Roshi before the cancer that killed him was when we were driving the three hours back to Minneapolis from Hokyoji monastery, near New Albin, Iowa. He was in the front passenger's seat and I was in the backseat behind the driver. We had just completed a kick-ass seven-day silent retreat, up at 5 A.M., asleep at ten in sleeping bags, the zendo a big canvas tent with early unexpected frost winding into the late September valley. A lot of energy had been building in our young bodies. Silence had been broken at the end of the week and soon after we were driving along the Mississippi River, heading north. Every once in a while someone in the car said something. I was mostly quiet, looking out the window.

Katagiri turned his head to look at me in the backseat. "Pretty good," he said. "Pretty good."

Never a lot of discussion with this Japanese teacher, but the understanding was transmitted.

I knew immediately what he was talking about. My transition was smooth. I was settled. I didn't go wild like a wild boar released from a pen. The final bell rang, a change occurred, and I rode it.

At the end of the True Secret Retreats, students can't seem to stop talking when we break silence in the early evening before supper and after Shabbat service. A small round table in the dining room has been designated the silent table in case students feel overwhelmed by the talking. No one goes there; maybe they can't tear themselves away, even if they long to, the chatter is so compelling. The din in the dining room is shattering.

For the last five years we've watched a film back in the zendo after the meal—this is a long way from the years of my Asian teacher. *Enlightenment Guaranteed, Fierce Grace, I'm Your Man, Être et Avoir, Tangled Up in Bob, Scent of a Woman, City Island, The Lover, In a Better World, The Quiet American, Gloomy Sunday* are a few of the choices. The movies serve as something constructive and engaging to quiet the talk compulsion, our urge to fill the new space inside that is both exhilarating and frightening. The film has worked well, but it is not enough.

Last June at the last dinner the pressure built. The student to my left, a longtime student who I am very fond of, was talking so much it was as though the ocean were pounding out of her. I had to control myself from not jumping up in the middle of the meal and screaming, *Shut up!*

Instead I stood up at the table and ate the rest of my meal this way just to get some distance from this student. I felt desperate.

"Natalie, why are you eating standing up?" she asked, her neck arched, head up, finally breaking her onrush.

"Oh, my back is aching," I lied.

Enough, I thought. I must do something.

The next retreat I devised this exercise for the zendo before silence is broken: Get into groups of three and when I ring the bell one person will talk for three minutes. During your talk you must pause four times, relaxing back into your body. The other two people, not talking, practice listening. For each round I will give a topic.

Okay, first round, tell what was most memorable about this week for you.

I walked around and eavesdropped.

Second round. What you learned about writing this week.

I remind them to pause, to breathe.

Third round. What you now know about sitting from this week.

Any pertinent topic can be made up. What you learned about eating, sleeping, breathing, listening, walking, desire this week.

I reminded them: When we break silence in the dining room, we are having *conversations*. One person speaks, one listens, both pause, the other speaks. Don't disregard all the care you practiced this week. And no monologues.

One student beseeched me, "How do you go home and relay your experience to your family?"

You don't, I responded. Keep quiet and practice what you learned. Go home and ask your wife how her week went—and listen. Remember, writing is 90 percent listening. If you listen well, it will convey to her a taste of your time away. She'll think, *Hmm, he really did learn something*.

Another student said, "I'm a minister. How do I bring this back? So many people rush at me all at once wanting, criticizing, demanding."

I turned to him: Remember the pauses we just practiced. Those pauses are a chance to come back to yourself, to breathe and feel the presence of your body.

I was determined to create a different last supper. I had another idea: I assigned the assistant every ten minutes to hit her knife on the water glass—ding—and we all had to be silent for three breaths right in the middle of our talk.

The clamor built in the first ten minutes after silence was broken. Ding. The sudden momentary silence was stunning. I could see the shock on many faces—where are we? How could the whole week be forgotten so easily in the intense running of our mouths? After the first big pause, the talking became much more settled, till I whispered to myself, *Pretty good, pretty good.*

Seven Attitudes of Mindfulness

Mindfulness means to be aware, awake. To be alive, attentive, receiving as we move through our day. Not brittle, blind, disjointed, out-of-touch, stressed, nervous, excited—or at least aware of these states and even having a bit of compassion for ourselves. This list is a reminder of another way to be in the world—really a relief, a way out of our distress.

1. Nonjudging

2. Patience

3. Beginner's mind

4. Trust

5. Nonstriving

6. Accepting

7. Letting go

These seven attributes are the state of mind advantageous for writing, sitting, walking. Also for approaching your employees, your boss, friend, lover, enemy. A way to carry yourself. And we can so easily forget. Put the list on your refrigerator.

PART THREE

Elaborations

Great robe of liberation

Field far beyond form and emptiness

Wearing Writing Practice teachings

Save all beings

—Slightly altered Zen verse

At the Beginning

What I want ultimately is for you to get out of the way. Let go of your little will and ideas and let something larger come through.

But, they protest, what if I want to write a novel?

Letting go is the best way.

And especially at the beginning, please let go of the novel. At least for two years just do writing practice. Find out what your real obsessions are. To write a novel takes a lot of committed energy over a long period of time. Those obsessions have that energy locked into them. To direct that energy toward a novel is a chance to transform an obsession, which diminishes your life, into a passion, something that enlarges your life.

Don't come at a novel from an intellectual idea, such as: I will write about a couple in love in World War II. You write the word *The* at the top of the page to begin your first sentence and then think, I don't want the novel to begin with *The*. You cross it out. An hour later twelve words are crossed out. You have no idea how to begin.

Instead, dive in with your odd obsessions—with whiskey, shopping, the Civil War, North Dakota, German cars, cats, old houses, and dry cereal and see what unfolds.

But Natalie, I hear, is this the way for a nice girl to write a book? I even hear this question in the voice of my grandmother, who definitely had no writing aspirations.

Grandma, I know no other way. You have to sweat, die, love, swim, catch the train, any way you can. I know, it's not what a nice Jewish girl looking for a husband should do. Forgive her. She'll probably never marry.

And let's take the student who says she just wants to write ten pages about her father. Can't she sit down and proceed?

Maybe so—and maybe not. Try it.

Writing is the act of discovery. If you want something alive, try this, too: write ten, ten-minute timed writings about your father during a week's time. The crazier the better. And if your mind goes to onions, trucks, ocean, straws, black shoes, don't fight it. Follow that trail. See where it leads. What seems illogical often can take you to deeper, more fertile ground about your father. Also don't worry if you repeat yourself.

Then a week later, reread all ten writings. Time lets the blood dry. You can see more clearly what you have written. You aren't as attached. The places where you were present almost glow off the page. It's obvious. Pull those out and see what you have. And the stuff that doesn't glow? Let it go. Our writing isn't that precious. Nothing glows? Dive in again the next week.

Not enough glows?

Come on. You know what to do: pick up the pen and write. You have to physically do it. Not *think* about it. An idea is not enough. You have to act.

At the same time, our lives have their own trajectory. No matter how hard you try to orchestrate your day, it seems to have its own composition. A large or different structure is operating through us. I'm not even talking of the divine here. We run into traffic, rain, our windshield wiper doesn't work, our son's teacher wants to meet with us, a rose is blooming outside our door, tuna is suddenly on sale at the local grocery, a headache, a moment we open the back door and flash on our dead brother, other people's needs, an unplanned phone call, our cat is sick—these are lucky interruptions. For some people, bombs drop, earthquakes rumble, a lump in the breast is discovered, or a hint is detected that our forty-year marriage is about to collapse—one morning your spouse smells of perfume, not yours. This is the daily, seemingly chaotic picture.

You also look back five, ten years and see there was an order to what unfolded or a cause and effect. It wasn't so out of the blue that you stopped speaking to an old friend or the country had a mortgage catastrophe.

So this is a tricky balance. While we have to show determination and muscle to get to our writing, to physically pick up the pen (or touch the keys), we also have to know that our little will can do little. Better to come to the page with the clouds and sun carrying us, the ache in our shoulder, last night's bad sleep, the bills unpaid, and the memory of our son's whistle. Don't cut anything out. Then, right from the beginning, we are beginning from a bigger place and we can let those things feed our writing. Rather than the bare idea to write a great novel and then the scratched-out idea of one on the page, let life, the very life you are living, inform you, support you. Don't fight what you think are obstacles.

Two weeks ago I taught a writing and yoga workshop. Susan Voorhees, my longtime yoga teacher, accompanied me. I threw the students a simple ten-minute assignment—*What do you want to write about?*

And I did it myself, moseying along, entering the assignment lazy and relaxed (maybe from the yoga):

> I don't have that much I want to write about but something does seem important to me—the years I was unknown and had my little VW Bug and drove across Nebraska. The times I dropped out, took off. I went to practice in St. Paul for a year and a half just as *Thunder and Lightning* was coming out and helped little with the publicity. I lived in a small apartment a block off Grand Ave. down from the River Gallery. Maybe that year and a half is an example of what I'm trying to tell them about writing practice. You begin with an idea of where you are going and once you begin it turns out all different.
>
> I went to St. Paul to study *The Book of Serenity,* help lead a practice period, sew robes and enter my old Japanese teacher's lineage. Instead I sat in a café that had really good cookies and

drank tea and began *The Great Failure* about how I discovered my wonderful Zen teacher was having sexual relations with some of his students. I tell my writing students to let writing do writing and I see how life does life. You go to do one thing and another comes up. Looking back eleven years later it seems totally appropriate how I spent my time. As I wrote I was living in the dark underbelly of Zen in America. Unknowingly, I came to St. Paul to face that. Late at night the yellow spring storms kept me up and I slept late into the mornings the days I didn't have to ring the bells at 5 A.M.

We want to do one thing that is our determined will and often we end up doing something else.

How did we get here? or anywhere? A seed was planted eons ago or we read a book in a bookstore in Boston and a friend died and suddenly you are in New Mexico, a place you've never been before and it's too dry here but you are writing the real thing your heart has always wanted to write. You follow the trail of your life and eventually your path reveals itself.

If you stay in relation to writing (rather than zoning out for six years) and you connect with writing friends, read, listen deeply, you will write what you want but most likely never the way you imagined it.

During the yoga week, I asked the students several times, How did you get here? A good writing topic has many levels. *I took a plane, then rented a car and drove along the Rio Grande Gorge.* How did you get here? *My mother was at Jones Beach in a black bathing suit. She was stunning at twenty-three with dark skin and a shock of kinky blue-black hair pulled back in a ponytail. My father was the lifeguard.* How did you get here? *My grandmother wanted to write and I wanted to write. We were both lost.*

How do we write? For me, it's almost a smell I taste far off, to my right, way down the line, in another county or a sound I hear in a fog, following a train moving fast through Kansas. That train is carrying the unresolved matter of my heart/mind and I've got to catch it, claim it, come to understand—gallop my pen after it.

Writing is magical, extraordinary, but we have to pick up the pen to run down the rails and catch that caboose. Determination, muscle, and a deep letting go get us back to that novel or that story about our fathers.

Story of Love

Okay, right in the middle of everything, without thinking, grab pen and paper (or keyboard): go, for a full hour, tell your story of love.

I did this at a retreat on the fourth day. The students had settled into the rhythm of the schedule and the silence and now I shattered it. Write for a full hour? They looked as though they'd just surfaced from underwater. Their eyes grew wide, jaws slacked, and then they grabbed for pens and the room hummed.

When they finished, several people read out loud: one wrote about three husbands, the second one growing to three hundred pounds; another wrote about a Virginia lover she tried to leave— he hunts and shoots, even uses bows and arrows, but oh is he sexy; someone else wrote about the land in Montana that had three years of drought, now this summer, floods, how her husband has left his scientific job at the university because global warming is beyond help and at least now fixing cars he can do something constructive; and a man from Texas wrote about the new girlfriend, who had two sons and he was slow to meet them and how he remembers the toothbrush sticking out of her back jeans pocket; and one even wrote about the love of wind, in seventeen parts.

That evening I asked them, *What did I find interesting about all the ones I heard?*

I often ask something like this. In one way it's inane. How would they know what I thought? But if you come to study writing from a certain writer, you are really coming to study that writer's mind. Not the incidentals of what they like for breakfast or who they married but the way they think and what they look for in writing, what they are cued in to, alert to. Knowing something of another writer's mind helps in forming and refining your own writer's mind. It's how we learn and transmit the writing lineage.

A stunned silence ensued, then a grinding of thoughts.

A new student called out, "Oh, come on, just tell us!"

"No, you wouldn't be able to receive it as well as if you found it yourself. Your effort makes you hungry, creates space in your mind to hear it."

I turned back to the group. "No one?"

Someone tried an answer. It wasn't close, but it's good to try. It heats you up.

Finally, I said, "I found it interesting that all of you stayed on the subject for the full time. If it was about a seemingly perfect childhood in New Zealand with Brethren religious parents, you went for it and told the full story. The writing didn't reflect as much the usual writing practice of following the mind as it jumps around, changing subjects. Eventually, writing practice leads to this, the harnessing of the force of your mind and galloping down one path but usually at this stage for an hour you'd jump around a lot more. Do you all see that?"

They nodded.

"It tells me you have become settled. I was interested in the structure of your minds, not in this case the actual stories—which were wonderful to hear.

"So let's go a little further. How could you extend this assignment? Take: tell me the story of—and expand its range."

They jumped right in:

Your story of sex

    joy

    coffee

    disappointment

    dessert

desert

getting in a lot of trouble

leaving

growing tomatoes

Which two on this list are different?

Coffee and growing tomatoes. More specific. Gives more direction. Good to be aware of that.

No one mentioned the story of loneliness. I add it here.

Writing is a communal act. "Come on, give me more," I said as I jotted down their list.

Story of grief

of shame

of feeling safe—go three minutes, someone joked.

Try any or all of these.

Then I looked up, pen in hand. "Very good. Chapter two of my book." I smiled broadly.

The new student didn't realize I was half teasing. She called out, "I'm going to steal from you, too, for my book."

"I hope you do—everyone else does."

The bell rang. We moved into silence for the rest of the night.

Kiss

Did you ever think about kissing? I bet you did—and do. If you think too hard on it, what an odd activity. What if you went to the Louvre and put a big smacker on Mona Lisa's face. What are we doing? What is this activity with our lips—and tongue—mixing saliva, touching teeth, close to another's face and nose. A sailor grabs an unknown woman in a white nurse's outfit in Times Square at the end of the war, bends her back, and plants his lips on hers. Are we crazy? What would a duck think? Or a clam? A tree?

Writers love to write about first kisses. Wouldn't you? What could you say that hasn't been said? What are the possibilities?

Let's look at *Ironweed* by William Kennedy. Page 155 in the paperback edition I found in the library (I used to own the book):

> . . . he perceived that a kiss is as expressive of a way of life as is a smile, or a scarred hand. Kisses come up from below, or down from above. They come from the brain sometimes, sometimes from the heart, and sometimes just from the crotch. Kisses that taper off after a while come only from the heart and leave the taste of sweetness. Kisses that come from the brain tend to try to work things out inside other folks' mouths and don't hardly register. And kisses from the crotch and the brain put together, with maybe a little bit of heart, like Katrina's, well they are the kisses that can send you right around the bend for your whole life.

Kennedy is first a little philosophical. He categorizes kisses. He examines the context, gets sure-footed before he dives in. How many kinds of kisses are there? And what a delight. We nod our heads up and down as we read.

And then Kennedy zeros in on his character's first kiss—on a lumber pile in Albany, New York. In this second paragraph Kennedy smashes through conventional grammar and punctuation, exactly the way a kiss does. No periods, one long, breathless sentence. No holding back.

Read it aloud:

> But then you get one like that first whizzer on Kibbee's lumber pile, one that come out of the brain and the heart and the crotch, and out of the hands on your hair, and out of those breasts that weren't all the way blown up yet, and out of the clutch them arms give you, and out of time itself, which keeps track of how long it can go on without you gettin' even slightly bored the way you got bored years later with kissin' almost anybody but Helen, and out of fingers (Katrina had fingers like that) that run themselves around and over your face and down your neck, and out of the grip you take on her shoulders, especially on them bones that come out of the middle of her back like angel wings, and out of them eyes that keep openin' and closin' to make sure that this is still goin' and still real and not just stuff you dream about and when you know it's real it's okay to close 'em again, and outa that tongue, holy shit, that tongue, you gotta ask where she learned that because nobody ever did that that good except Katrina who was married and with a kid and had a right to know, but Annie, goddamn, Annie, where'd you pick that up, or maybe you been gidzeyin' heavy on this lumber pile regular (No, no, no, I know you never, I always knew you never), and so it is natural with a woman like Annie that the kiss come out of every part of her body and more, outa that mouth with them new teeth Francis is now looking at, with the same lips he remembers and doesn't want to kiss anymore except in memory (though that could be subject to change), and he sees well beyond the mouth into a primal location in this woman's being, a location that evokes in him not only the memory of years but decades and even more, the memory of

epochs, aeons, so that he is sure that no matter where he might have sat with a woman and felt this way, whether it was in some ancient cave or some bogside shanty, or on a North Albany lumber pile, he and she would both know that there was something in each of them that had to stop being one and become two, that had to swear that forever after there would never be another (and there never has been, quite), and that there would be allegiance and sovereignty and fidelity and other such tomfool horseshit that people destroy their heads with when what they are saying has nothing to do with time's forevers but everything to do with the simultaneous recognition of an eternal twain, well sir, then both of them, Francis and Annie, or the Francises and Annies of any age, would both know in that same instant that there was something between them that had to stop being two and become one.

Such was the significance of that kiss.

Francis and Annie married a month and a half later.

Years ago when I first discovered Kennedy's book I read this passage aloud at retreats in New York and Boston and Madison, Wisconsin. And recently, at least ten years later, I pulled it out again in front of a group in Charleston, South Carolina. That's the wonderful thing about teaching something you love—you get to repeat until it's in your own body and brain, till you don't know if you are William Kennedy or Kennedy is you. Things become fluid. *War and Peace* by Natalie Goldberg. *Madame Bovary* by Natalie Goldberg. You breathe the author's breath when you read the words aloud and you swim in their minds. That is how writing is passed on.

When I read this passage in Charleston, where two rivers surround and embrace that great southern town, then converge in the sea, I almost fell forward, no sentence structure to hold me up, almost collapsed to the floor, lips first. Just the reading aloud of it is a wonderful experience.

Who has ever paid much attention to Albany, New York? Kennedy lived there and honored it, not in just this one book but in a trilogy. You don't have to live in Paris or Big Sur or New York to write. It's in the details of the town you live in that give you your place. From what I hear Albany is a broken-down city with not much glamour, mostly lower- and middle-class working people and lots of unemployed. Cracks on the sidewalk, empty lots, and long, unforgiving winters. But now it's also become a literary place. Beautiful novels have been written about it. And because Kennedy exposed its marrow and gumption, I want to see the place, drive slowly up and down its streets, preferably in spring, preferably in a fat Buick circa 1959, blue, with all the time in the world.

I did fly into Albany once. It was the quickest route to a bookstore in Vermont and I was picked up by a driver who lived in Albany. He let me sit in the front seat.

Go ahead, Nat, I urged myself. "Do you get a chance to read much—with all the driving you do?"

"Not much." He shook his head. He was about middle fifties, two grandchildren, a wife, three sons, he told me. I heard about his oldest son being out of work, about the summer he broke his ankle and couldn't drive.

Seemingly out of the blue, I asked, "Ever read a novel by William Kennedy?"

His face lit up. "No," he shook his head. "But I know about him. We all do. We are so proud. I should read it sometime."

I had a real connection now. I asked about his favorite hangout when he was a kid, what kind of trees lined the streets, did his junior high have windows. I asked, are there a lot of drunks on the Albany streets? Francis, the main character, was one and often almost homeless. I could ask anything now because we were in the range of literature, the imagination, and my driver, Harry, knew it, too. Our conversation had a context.

An author can do this for you. You land in a place but it is no longer remote, vague. You can be lit with curiosity because you know something about the inside of it.

For a long time Kennedy couldn't get any publisher interested in *Ironweed*. Somehow finally the manuscript landed on the desk of the great American novelist Saul Bellow—probably a friend knew a friend, who knew a friend, and he was generous enough to read it.

Bellow called his publisher and said, if you don't publish this, I'll never publish a book with you again.

Ironweed won the Pulitzer the year it came out.

Let's consider this structure Kennedy gave for the kiss. First examining the different types, then plunging into the real experience. Let's pick something we have a passion for—a football player, our last lover, a cup of coffee, a thick shake, snowboarding, peace, lips, knees.

Let's do it like he did. First categorize it. For instance, what different kinds of running shoes are there, how do they work—what can you say new about them? Then pause, let it rip—tell us about a specific pair, yours. Where have you been with them, why, what, who—throw in the whole universe, what it's like to run, walk, to have a foot, to be on pavement, grass, tennis court. Break down category, idea, boundary. Follow your own trail out into the rain.

Things to Draw

This summer I visited the Aspen Art Museum and found *642 Things to Draw* (Chronicle Books) in their bookstore. No author. No instructions. A thick, blocky tome. School bus bright yellow cover. Blank pages, whole or divided into halves, quarters, or thirds. And in the upper left of each section, a single noun, remember those? A person, place, or thing. Something to draw, something you can get your teeth around. Sometimes a phrase, "an uneventful street." The book felt so meaty (excuse me, vegetarians), so full of protein and possibility. I snapped it up and took it home.

And I brought it to two retreats. I had an idea: What if we drew with words?

But first, for fun and to warm up: Try actually drawing these in your writing notebook. You don't have to be Michelangelo. Just use your pen in different motions, spend maybe one to three minutes on each:

a gun

root beer

a bus stop

a truck

a tennis racquet

an iris

a haircut

an Easter bonnet

a screwdriver

fried eggs

a piece of wheat toast

Jack Kerouac called his short poems "Sketching," getting down in a moment what was before him. And the thing about words is they can travel anywhere. What's before you is your foot up on the coffee table, tell about that, but what's before you is also what's behind you, your past, and what you do not know, your future, and everything in between, especially all your nutty thoughts. So drawing with words has great dimensions—this is always true with writing. You can go anywhere, also crazy. So instead we have this nitty-gritty book. Take a noun. That noun can anchor us, a place to begin.

"Pudding, go," I told the retreat. "You have five minutes, draw it with words." Five minutes was half the time of our normal writing practice. The students galloped out of the gate with every fiber concentrated on this central noun, narrowing down the focus, keeping it lean, direct, connected to the object, and simultaneously springing open the range and the senses. They ignored roadblocks, got to it, forcing anything in them to come out, go, go, go.

PUDDING

My-Tee-Fine from a box, chocolate, of course, forget vanilla, caramel and raspberry though they are good too. This is 1959. Open box and shake out powder in saucepan, mix with two cups of milk—in the Fifties they were concerned with nutrition—milk mixed with powdered chemicals. I stir and the smell becomes home, all good things, the trees outside the bay window, clothesline where my grandpa stands in his leather tan body and navy blue shorts, hanging sheets, a stogie cigar unlit in corner of mouth.

We did more rounds:

SPOON

Spoon me in bed. You come from behind and form your shape to my shape, your legs behind mine, slightly bent and your chest to my back, under the covers, summer night screen door open, cricket click and the damn four chihuahuas next door barking in middle hours at roving raccoons, who eat ever so skillfully with their delicate paws, my green grapes at the perfect moonlit moment of ripeness under the heavy green leaves of the arbor. They don't eat the tomatoes, not yet ripe, and they wait for the raspberries to grow deep red and the strawberries under their low leaves coming from first white flowers, and the air grows colder at four A.M.

A SARDINE TIN

Those small elegant thin fish lying side by side, almost forever in the deep breathless dark of oil. You open the can and finally the long patience of industry lets out its bouquet—it was years ago these fish died and now live again. Bury me with a can of sardines so forty years after my death, when I'm hungry, I'll wake to nourishment and the hidden scent of unlit kerosene lamps in the exposed valley of oily heaven.

Give me two cans, my need will be great, more ravenous than two nickels on the pavement, longing to be picked up and pocketed.

PERFUME

Smell of petroleum, put behind the earlobes of the damaged, to entice the unknowing, in shelves of hope. Oh, legends of sailors.

Oh, women in lace. Oh, hunger for something ineffable, following the flowering scent around street corners and seaports, wanting something we don't know what, driven for sex and future generations. Perfume ensures our continuation, spells trouble and hope, is as old as Paris, takes no prisoners. More potent than smelly cheese, more listing than a willow, on the backs of workers the smell carries us through the broken generations, hungry for bacon, gardenias, a woman's thighs, alcohol in the night.

A CUPCAKE

I'm done, no more writing for me, and no more coffee, no more anything but socks for my feet and a bad burp at the back of the throat, a tired ok but older now and cannot push quite as fast. Back to old poetry, the root of all evil and smoke. I should have used smoke in the poem about perfume, but it's here instead after the fire dies out and we are alone again the next morning tired but our old hearts still bursting for more, while even the hands growing cold. So we eat a cupcake.

No place to hide. You don't even know what you wrote. We coined it "Bullet Writing."

I flip open the pages of the yellow book. Here's some more possibilities for writing: *first love, electricity*. How do you draw electricity? It must be concrete but words in their very nature are not concrete. And things in their very nature are not what they seem. *A real estate agent, vitamins, a doily, an office park, a Q-tip, chips and dip, cheese, an afternoon, leftovers, a flamingo, dice, a typewriter* (use your imagination, conjure what one could look like), *a paper coffee cup, cat whiskers, a trolley car, a football, a phone booth* (use your imagination), *an accordion.*

Though no author signed his or her name, as I page through the book I get a feeling for the person who created it, even in these nouns. Urbane, connected to society, caring about human, daily life. He or she, let's call her Alberta, walked around a city and picked out, noted things she saw. Jotted them down. "Trolley car" gives it away. She walked up and down the streets of that hilly city, San Francisco, and then had the good grace to step completely out of the way. Not even an introduction, only draw, however you like. No delicious epilogue, a culmination, an outcome. You just do what you do. Alberta found 642 things and she was finished, didn't round the number out.

What is around you that can be seen? Look. Don't miss it. Right now in early autumn everything is giving itself up, ripe raspberries, last tomatoes, sunflowers, cosmos, squash, chilies, soft air, a slight twitch of cold in the early morning hour before the sun rises, a smell of winter if you turn your head quickly at the corner, vines clinging for the last moment. Everything is rising up to meet us. Don't turn your back. Be here, even when it aches. Acknowledge what has been given.

The List

Yes, there is the grocery list. That in itself can be interesting—if you read someone else's. But also there is the list in writing which is delightful to create. It's not necessarily set out in a column—it can run across the page—but it can call up all you know about something.

Try these opening lines and create lists. Keep it to specifics:

> What do you carry?
>
> What are the simplest things of all?
>
> Before I leave, I want to tell you . . .
>
> What remains of _____ (fill in a person or place) in me?

These topics give you good first lines to enter your list. Without that the list is just a list, no matter how odd or unique the details may be. The opening line is what glues it together. For instance, look at this list: a canyon in Arizona, the town dump, the ballpark, the Big Horn Mountains, Route 66, a shopping mall, seat 23D on a flight to Los Angeles, a soldier's grave in Virginia, the suburban backyard. What's it about? Here's the entry line: "This is a book of poems in which the poet simply is carried away by a particular place in America"—and then the above list follows. Do you see how the list makes sense now? It's from Garrison Keillor's introduction to *Good Poems, American Places,* where he goes on to say that the poems in this anthology are "memoirs of the place in that moment." Lovely way to look at poems.

Let's look at a poem by Allen Ginsberg:

A STRANGE NEW COTTAGE IN BERKELEY

All afternoon cutting bramble blackberries off a tottering
brown fence
under a low branch with its rotten old apricots miscellaneous
under the leaves,
    fixing the drip in the intricate gut machinery of a new
    toilet;
    found a good coffeepot in the vines by the porch, rolled a
big tire out of the scarlet bushes, hid my marijuana;
    wet the flowers, playing the sunlit water each to each,
returning for godly extra drops for the stringbeans and daisies;
    three times walked round the grass and sighed absently:
    my reward, when the garden fed me its plums from the
form of a small tree in the corner,
    an angel thoughtful of my stomach, and my dry and love-
lorn tongue.

Can you see how this poem by Ginsberg is mostly structured by
an ornate list? And notice how the title "A Strange New Cottage in
Berkeley" in this case is the entry into the list.

The list gives you a structure. The opening line can make it literature.

Try these entry lines. If you get lost, keep coming back, rewrite
the entry line and keep going:

> I want to tell you . . .
>
> I'm thinking of . . .
>
> I'm looking at . . .
>
> How I came to love my life . . .

Lists can be simple but I'll tell you, they are one of the true back-
bones of writing.

Loving a Place

Early Saturday evening at the end of February I stop in Minneapolis for two nights on my way to Bismarck, North Dakota. Amazingly, Delta charges two hundred dollars less if I make this stop on my way from Albuquerque.

I stand outside baggage claim with my suitcase, waiting for my old friend Erik to drive by and pick me up. The cold is so bitter, it's almost exciting. You cannot take it for granted. The traffic control man greets me as he chases away a Ford parked too long at the entrance.

"Wait a minute!" I shout, my breath a fog in front of me. "You have no hat or gloves. Are you crazy?"

"I don't even feel it anymore." He gives me a big proud grin. "Lived here all my life. If it gets to twenty below I put on my wool cap." Oh, yes, the Minnesotans and their love and defiance of long winter.

I look hard trying to see the drivers in their cars. I'm not sure what kind Erik is driving. Finally he pulls up in a big white Toyota. I fling my ridiculously heavy bag for such a short visit into the backseat and hop into the front. We maneuver our way along streets made one lane by the snow this winter that has broken records and is plowed eight feet high on either side.

Erik grins as he glances over at me with my eyes wide, jaw ajar, breath held in. "Oh, I love it," he says.

The next day when we pass a Wells Fargo parking lot that has been plowed all through the long weeks of December, January, and February and the snow is easily twelve feet high and we crane our necks to look up, my friend Carol says, "You know, this is how an ice age begins. So much snow, summer can't melt it."

I believe her. I think maybe this is what love is, the blatant truth of it—something raw, no matter how you try to civilize it. And, believe me, Minneapolis tries for civilization, with its endless coffee shops you can sit in all day, Garrison Keillor and Louise Erdrich have two hearty bookstores and a huge used bookstore Magers & Quinn sits near the corner of Hennepin and Thirty-First around the corner from Lucia's, where you can get croissants and cookies, all kinds of delicious baked goods, because it is the heartland where wheat comes from and they know how to bake.

Carol, who was brought up on a North Dakota farm, and I go to the Minneapolis Art Institute, which, since I was there last, has added a new wing. It gets bigger and bigger, extending itself out into the barren cold. It's warm in here and we get to look at culture—oil paintings from France, Buddha statues, photos from Minnesota artists who left Minnesota. And then passing through the galleries we come upon a glass window, and we look out on bare black trees against dirty snow across the street from the institute, the sky a deep dirty gray in the dwindling four-in-the-afternoon light. We are very far north and the two of us stare. The most real picture of all.

"Well, this is pretty," Carol says sarcastically. She has had it with winter. "Like the ones when you were here in the late seventies."

This winter Carol's roof was so bad, she had to fill her old nylon stockings with salt and throw them up there. The salt melted a rivulet in the thick mass of ice and gave her a foothold, a way in to break up the solid sheet before the whole thing collapsed into the house.

I ask Carol, a prominent dermatologist in the Twin Cities, "Why don't you hire someone before you break your neck?"

"I just can't—if I can do it myself," she says. When the roof leaks, she's up there; when the plumbing's bad, she's down there. This is an old joke between us. Women from North Dakota are known for their strength and independence. When the men went to war the women had to do the farm work and when the men came home a lot of them weren't right in the head so the women continued to do all the heavy labor and this legacy has continued.

I realize that half the conversations here with old friends are about the weather and I listen in fascination. This is not boring, idle chatter. It is immediate sharing.

One friend tells me three people in her neighborhood slipped on the ice and fractured their hips. "One slipped and hit her head on an ice pack along the road and since then doesn't know who she is."

"In this weather wouldn't you want to forget yourself?" I chortle.

I bundle up and leave my friend Erik's house early on Sunday morning to walk around Lake Calhoun three blocks away. I have the clothes now to keep warm, a thick down parka, heavy wool hat, double knit mittens, silk long underwear, and good boots. When I lived here in my early thirties, I drove a beige Volkswagen Bug with no heat. On my way to teach at Central High School, driving across town on the highway at sixty miles an hour with the rest of the 7 A.M. morning traffic, I had to roll open my window and scrape the frost from the windshield so I could see out. The temperature dived to twenty below on December second and never came up till spring. And spring came slowly throughout April, till you believed it wouldn't come again into the green of May.

Maybe this Sunday morning walk is finally my peace with the horror of this weather. I don't even seem to mind it. I have a wool scarf wrapped around my face and I'm not sure if it's eleven degrees, nine degrees, or four degrees below zero. At a certain point it doesn't matter. It's cold cold, like pouring cream into cream. You can't separate it out. A couple walks by with a cocker spaniel who has boots on his feet. Even a dog can't bear this ice plastered to the walks.

A few years back, Erik, a staunch Minnesotan, showed me how he sat zazen out on frozen Lake Calhoun. Standing on the ice, he first bowed in the four directions and then settled himself on the cushion on top of a mat he lugged out on the lake. Then as the sun was setting and he sat stone still, he said, "It's quite pleasant and I hope someday it will catch on."

Two women jog past me, then later a man with a dog on a leash;

otherwise, I have the place to myself. I pick up my pace feeling the tips of my fingers freezing. I can't believe how much love I feel for this place with no logic to it. Sure I met my great Zen teacher here and lived a few blocks away from him for six years and, yes, I learned a lot about writing here, teaching in poet-in-the-schools and then resident writer for two years in a multiracial, multiethnic elementary school and then finally winning a big in-state fellowship that brought me to Israel and that recognized me as a writer. But stopping by a hackberry and staring across the flat white surface of the lake as cars at my back speed by, I understand love has no reason, makes no sense.

Finally I didn't belong here, just as some of my best loves were not practical to live with or marry, but spoke to a part of me that yearned to be met. And as the years go by I remember them with all the unsheltered love I couldn't manage to tame. Even though no one would call Minneapolis a wild place, besides its winters, for me, a second-generation Jewish girl from Brooklyn, it was my American frontier. I met people who grew up on Iowa farms, close to that sprawling wide American river, the Mississippi. I watched as people dug holes in the ice and fished and went to summer cabins in the north of their state. I come back to Minneapolis as a seminal home where I have no family and no roots, like a stranger in a strange place.

I've written about Minnesota a lot, struggling to escape what I thought was a weird attachment. Most Minnesotans think I hate their state. They are wrong. When I write about a place at all, even if I make fun of it, it's because it's stuck to my heart.

My friend Miriam says I have a jones for place. Some people love cars, old houses, the cut and line of clothes. What does our obsession tell us about ourselves?

When I think of my mother, she was mad for beauty—in cups, plates, sweaters, shoes, coats, hats, placemats, carpets, couches, lamps, curtains, earrings, rings, candy dishes, saucers, knives, forks, spoons. It was her entrée into a bigger world, her entrance to happiness, her escape from ordinary squalor. I wanted her happiness to be us, me and my sister. But she couldn't focus on us. Color, texture, form is what lit her.

On Monday I continued on to North Dakota. I ain't seen nothin' yet of the cold. The hour-and-a-half ride from Bismarck west to Dickinson near the Montana border is a barren flat frozen plain that meets the sky at the horizon with nothing to break the view. We are moving through a white vacuum. The car shakes from the wind whipping across the highway. Now I have really stepped into another world as the car bumps along in the parking lot of the Ramada, where I'm dropped off. The ice on the ground is a solid two feet deep and wavy on top.

"It's too cold to use salt right now," the kind professor, who has written a book on Mark Twain and one on Charles Johnson, and who has picked me up, explains.

The lobby is dark and thick with the smell of cigarettes. No anti-smoking laws have reached here yet. Oil has been discovered on the land around Dickinson and in the last year several ranchers have become millionaires, but I'm told they keep their money close. The whole state has less than a million people.

I am visiting the students at the Dickinson State University. They are open, ready, and a bit lazy. They expect me—the visiting writer—to entertain them while they sit back for a free ride.

"Okay, everyone," I command. "Stand up and take off your shoes."

I show them how to stand like a flamingo on one foot. "We have to balance—not only our body but our mind. One thought and we topple."

Then we bend over and touch our toes, "for our old backs," I joke to these students in their late teens and early twenties.

"Okay, you can go back to your seats. We will go around, say your name, where you were born, and one food you like."

Claire says, "Chinese food."

"Be specific. What kind?"

She makes a face—she doesn't know.

After Mexican food, mashed potatoes, steak, hamburgers, one girl from Montana says, "Applesauce," and we all laugh.

"Okay, why did that make us laugh? Writers examine the mind." I stopped the class from going on to the next person.

The young woman next to her says, "Because applesauce is simple; you don't expect it."

I nod, then notice she is wearing Bermuda shorts. It is eleven below zero outside. I point to her legs. "Are you crazy?"

She tosses one shoulder forward. "I was brought up here."

"So you defy winter?"

"Naw," she said smiling. She loves the attention.

On the last day we list things we remember from childhood.

> My baby sister chewing on my shoe
>
> The goat in the kitchen when the temperature went to fifty below
>
> How my father whistled
>
> A boy named Joseph who died in second grade
>
> The school bus pulling up and the wide swing of the door

The next day two professors drive me over to the Theodore Roosevelt National Park. It is ten below and on the distant hills we see wild bison and a little farther, wild horses.

"Do you want to hear the romantic or the historical explanation of those horses?"

"Both," I say.

"Well, the first is that they are the descendants of Sitting Bull's horses, the ones he let loose when he knew it was the end."

"I like that." I look off into the wide, cold expanse.

"The historical version is they are farm horses that were no longer useful."

"So they became wild and beautiful," I add.

I leave North Dakota and think, *You scratch the surface just a little and you can find realized mind everywhere.* But those kids in the class, those sweet teachers, don't know they are awake, or how lovely they are. For most of us, "awake" isn't even a quality we look for. We are busy with earning a living, getting good grades, anticipating spring break. Awake is another country; yet it's our job to recognize that country, to realize love of place can be a beginning point, a reflecting back, a map of our longing and hope.

A Long Chapter on a Short Practice

A Week of Writing in a Café

Stare, pry, listen, eavesdrop.
Die knowing something. You are
not here long.

—WALKER EVANS, 1960

S ometime, you might want to try a short practice: go to the same
coffee shop for seven days in a row, the same hour, the same
seat and record what's in front of you, what you hear, see, smell,
taste. No interpretation.

I've mentioned this short practice to retreat students, but it
hasn't seemed to stir anyone but me. I decided finally to do it.

At the end of November, the day after Thanksgiving, I committed myself to going to the Tea House on Canyon Road at noon
every day for seven days and to write straight for twenty minutes
"what was in front of my face," grabbing what I could of over-
heard conversations, people at tables, people coming and going. I'll
admit it would have been more efficient to bring a laptop (they have
Wi-Fi) but I'm an old dog and I snatched what I could of the action
with pen and paper. I set it up as a short exploratory practice, just
to see how it felt.

The hard part was my immediate resistance on the first day.
Already I didn't want to do it. I had a stomachache. I didn't want to be

in a café where everyone was eating. Choosing noon was impossible; it was the middle of the day. What was I thinking? Better first thing in the morning. And then I thought, *This is a beginning writer's activity*. It sounded so attractive when I proposed it. *I can't learn anything new,* I told myself. That Friday, the first day after a holiday, the place was filled with visiting family and friends. Here I was again alone, writing. I fell into an old pit—the lonely writer. Why didn't I become a funeral director, a plumber, a short-order cook? Not this again.

Natalie, shut up. You said you were going to do it, you're here the first morning, follow through. Stop being so dramatic.

I half bit the bullet. Only one day did I get there exactly on time and I missed one day in the middle but made it up at the end, continuing consecutively till I hit seven.

But now three weeks later—I hate to admit it—though there was intense resistance I learned a lot. First, I see the old girl can still show up. Second, I find myself thinking a bit about the people I wrote about, even in such a brief encounter. I also find myself more attuned to people's conversations. Just this past week at a True Secret Retreat, as I led the group slow walking out of the zendo into the courtyard, I heard two people speaking loudly outside the kitchen. Normally I would ignore this or include it as part of general sound or on a bad day be annoyed that the staff didn't respect silence. But because of the café practice, my senses were piqued. What was their relationship? I realized the loudness was an exalted state. The woman laughed full-throated at everything he said. Why, they were flirting. I felt more alive in being alive to them.

Below are some of the recordings from the Teahouse:

Friday Nov. 27th

12:05 at Teahouse on Canyon Road. Mad dash to get here at exactly noon day after Thanksgiving. I've been wanting to do this ever since I mentioned it to students. Here goes:

"It takes eighteen minutes in rice cooker."

"It's rice and maple and cream, Harvey. It's too rich for whole foods."

"I would prefer a smaller portion."

"Do you get your cholesterol checked?"

"I need a smaller portion."

"My overall number was 249."

Baby with white cap is carried out.

Man in gold framed glasses, red ski jacket carries his cup to bussing bin. He turns around and his belly is busting zipper of jacket. Wilting fig plant in corner of opening to next room.

Young man with black brillo hair sits next to me reading thick book, I glance at title in upper left, *Life Itself,* has on jeans and sips last liquid in bottom of cup. He gets up to get another cup and turns over his book. By Bill Bryson. He comes back, nothing in cup, I assume line too long at counter two rooms away. Checks hand computer, goes back to book, leans against edge of table.

Woman, who earlier gave high cholesterol count, now says, "Your lamb was delicious, didn't have gamey taste. I did discover one goat cheese, no, Shepherd's cheese, didn't have gamey taste but other night I looked at it and it looked very red and I couldn't eat it."

Woman with purse slung over right shoulder, carrying in left hand a cone in front of face with pink ice cream walks out.

"Well if you talk about colonoscopies with eating food it's gross."

Woman who works here, in pale gray sweater and jeans, calls out: "Where's number 13?"

And across from me in other room is woman sitting very erect typing on computer on lap. Burnt orange sweater, plant behind her.

Man next to me checks his hand computer again after looking at movie schedule in The Reader.

He says to me after putting on hat and gloves: "I don't know if I want to go out there. It's cold."

I ask him: "What kind of computer?"

"Motorola."

"How's the book?"

"If you like science, it's great."

"Are you a student?"

"Part-time at UNM and work part-time at Santa Fe Institute."

"Oh, with Geoffrey West?"

He nods.

"If you stand in the sun it's not too cold." He leaves.

"I had a Jewish mother who was so strict. With my father, I could do no wrong."

"I can't think of the word—oh, 'resent'—some people so resent how they were brought up, they go in the opposite direction."

"I have the world's tightest sneakers."

She sticks out her foot with black sneaker. "I have a lot of Mephistos."

Saturday Nov. 28th, 12:10

Today I'm ten minutes late to my practice goal. Two days after Thanksgiving and I'm slurping Kombucha, a fermented tea, for my stomach and it's beautiful and warm and I want to sit for these twenty minutes outside and write, but I said "same place" meaning "same seat." I'm at same café. Couldn't get exact same seat but a round table next to it.

A couple's at the table I sat at yesterday, holding hands across the tabletop. Man with light gray sweatshirt has back to me. Woman—both in thirties—wearing dark teal tee-shirt saying, Rock 'n Roll, Las Vegas 2009—has just lifted clear glass of tea to mouth. Now she leans head in hand and listens to boyfriend, who is talking about his dad "is the same way. A little blurriness in back of head and eyes get tired and I'm shutting down. So last night no brainer I went home."

"You said that."

"Well, in future I would definitely have gone." His words are fast. He wants her to understand. "Now you can see it's not all about me. I just don't trust. I trust you."

She is leaning forward and shaking her head. She has thin penciled-in eyebrows and straight shoulder length brown hair and filed fingernails, not painted a color.

"So now you know my intentions," he says.

He wants so much from her. Come back to me, understand, his tone is saying.

And now she is talking, clipped, about a girl they both encountered last night. Edge of defense in voice.

And a couple with baby in pink jacket wheeled in carriage crosses path.

I reach for Kombucha. I have not ordered anything. I'll leave a dollar in tip jar. Passed order station and went right to table, already late, after noon.

"Absolutely not," she says now.

She laughs. "Noo" and the word has three syllables.

"So this is how I feel. We don't need to take time—unless you want to. Tell me right now."

She answers in low voice I cannot hear.

Now they begin arguing.

"I never say things like that. I introduced you to my family. You said your family never does Thanksgiving."

"My mom doesn't do Thanksgiving."

At table kitty corner to them a couple lean over very thick books and notebooks and taking notes. He is wearing black glasses.

Chef walks in door with white apron and baseball cap. Looks around. Navy and white striped tee-shirt.

Sunday, skipped.

Monday Nov. 30th

Didn't mean to skip yesterday but was up very late the night before. I'm not sure I was happy missing yesterday. Wasn't my goal to do it straight for seven days? It didn't seem that hard. It's the noon every day that is hard. Well, it is Monday now. And I'm here a half hour early. Ready and eager. So maybe skipping that day is ok.

Exactly noon at the Tea House.

Two men dressed in black sit by fireplace at round table. Big crosses hang from their necks. One looks tough with a black cap, beard, deep rings under his eyes, the other more fragile and in a priest dress, long blond beard, bald head—I realize I have to be careful, not keep looking up at them. The tough one looked at me and I'm leaning toward them, trying to hear. Priest talks, other listens but can't hear clearly what is being said. I hear the words Christian, church, Hindu. Something happened to tough one, "I wanted to make an issue of it. A strong faction in this town that is New Age. Most of them I know personally are covering . . ." Can't hear.

Woman to left in light gray shirt; turquoise coat smashed against back of chair. She is looking at computer and kitty corner at next table is someone I can't see but has dark green shirt.

I ordered a half sandwich and vegan mushroom soup that is delicious but I'm freezing, my left hand tucked between legs.

Tough one continues to talk in monotone and priest just said one sentence.

La Bamba is suddenly played but I'm not sure from where.

Man with green shirt just stood up to go to bathroom, but bathroom locked, went back to seat. He has gray hair, balding, wears jeans.

Tough one: "I want to make amends. I made some mistakes in my reaction, need to help. It was an oversight of mine . . ." Can't hear again.

Asian couple walks in this room and walks out looking for table.

Hate this room, cold and the seats are hard. Tough man glances at me. Cannot look at them.

Two men come in back door heavily dressed for winter. Conversation throughout place is heating up. Sharp cough from other room. Pale yellow painted walls, in corner three piles of plastic glasses stacked up next to water container, then knives, forks, spoons wrapped with napkins. Then bottle of tabasco and two sugar bottles and a wooden box of sugar substitute, that I also notice on my table. Packets of turbinado sugar.

Priest talks very calmly, doesn't mean he is calm, just schooled in it. He says "huge disaster."

"I dumped on you."

Priest nods.

Woman with computer has gone to bathroom. Now green man goes and the priest and tough man still in intense talking. It's where the energy in this room is. "I desire to be understood." Tough man's face is skewered, right corner of mouth up—he is intently listening to priest, so I glance at them. He has corn chip in hand.

"Can I question in respectful way?" he asks.

If you ask my opinion, which no one is, tough guy is giving too much power away to priest and should trust himself more.

Tuesday Dec. 1st, 12:14

Cannot seem to make noon no matter what. In 1990 right when Gulf War began Rob Wilder and I sat every day at noon in the Santa Fe Plaza with a sign, Sitting for Peace in the Middle East. It was sometimes at skidding breakneck speed to get there on time but seemed absolutely necessary. It makes a difference if you do something with someone else. Being on time is more imperative.

People ask me now what my day is like—what they are really asking is when do I write and I can't tell them.

Woman just walked through this room—by the way it's empty. Only me sitting next to the fire and distant reggae. Woman who walked through is back and she has terrible smelling perfume on. She mutters, "I'll sit over there" and comes near fire and next to me. Oh, shit, the perfume stinks. They just brought her covered cup of something—I can't say tea. She's wearing face powder and lipstick. I bet she doesn't live here. You can always tell the New Mexicans from the tourists.

Maybe I'll ask her when I'm done and let you know but if I ask now it will stop this writing. Another way I know besides make-up and perfume, she's eating a grilled sandwich with wheat bread. Everyone in Santa Fe has a gluten or wheat allergy. We are all allergic. It's a sick place. Don't move here.

Did I say paper lanterns hang from the ceiling with fake Chinese characters? Would it kill them to write in real Chinese characters? The floor is wood and dirty, crumbs under the table and the service is very slow and cramped at the ordering counter but the food is very good and when it is warm it's heaven to sit outside at the edge of Canyon Road. I never come here and sit inside, so why did I choose this for end of November through a lonely Thanksgiving weekend? The sun is pouring through the window onto my back and I see the shadow of my head on the table and the pen's shadow skidding across the page. Suddenly everything seems sweet, like the old days of writing in a café. You and your mind and the world and a Perrier I'm sipping.

Someone tripped in the next room and a howl, a laugh and I look up. A woman sits down on the couch in next room wearing a beige baseball cap. I bet she doesn't live here either. Only tourists on a Tuesday after Thanksgiving dribble in and this lone writer writing in her green notebook.

Ok, I give in and ask the perfume woman, "Do you live here?"

"Yes," she said. "And you do too. You used to live in Taos."

"Oh so you know who I am?"

"Do you miss Taos?"

It's turned on me now. I was all wrong. "Yes," I say, "but I love it here."

A big man enters. "Are you Patricia? We should move so we don't disturb her. She is writing."

"It's ok I'm winding down." And then I add, "And if I wasn't I could incorporate your conversation." We both laugh.

You see, I don't know shit. Who lives here and who doesn't.

Wednesday Dec. 2nd, noon

I realize it takes time to settle in to a routine. Today I just slid in and didn't fight it. Yesterday in conversation with perfume woman she says she even studied with me two different weeks up in Taos ten years ago. She was lovely and forget about my opinions, make-up and perfume. All this is deep study of the dumb too critical mind. I smell something delicious that the kitchen is cooking. I think salmon with pecans that I did not order. I'm at round table with back heated by fire. In corner with back toward me is woman, short gray hair, and maroon and orange colors of Buddhist nun. She is sitting with man with foreign accent, big smile, she laughs. He has uncombed curly hair and bright blue eyes, black jacket. Cannot hear what he is saying only part of the accent comes across.

Very large woman sits down at table between me and nun and holds cell phone to ear, has right arm draped over chair back next to her. She looks unhappy, a face full of consternation as she listens to her messages, then sighs and gazes out window. She sips at green bottle of Perrier. Her friend joins her and talks with her hands.

"I think the key thing to remember. He wants to accommodate his guests who want to go to Taos when they visit Bishop

Lodge. He probably told you a lot and you have to think about what he said."

"When you say a package, what do you mean?" I can hear the big one but not her friend.

Now both of them are looking at their computers. "You know my dogs do not like me on the computer. My pit bull growls."

Woman across leans on hand. Wears heavy eye make-up and lipstick. I will not guess anything about her.

"I don't have to sell Taos. Everyone wants it."

Server comes over from back room to add more wood to fire.

Woman is frowning now, arms crossed waiting for food—or drink.

On serving island when I walked in read front page of *New York Times*. Riots in Italy because tuitions have been raised. Europe hustling to keep economy going, Berlin while digging for subway unearths sculptures hidden during Nazi rage at modern art.

Woman still not served. Slight smile. Here comes her quiche.

Only person I can hear is big woman, who says, "I'm an old social worker and can't help noticing people glaring at us and I hope they are nicer to their guests."

"Maybe next time," surfaces from man with nun.

Woman across reaches for salt. Has large glass of water with straw. She blows on food on fork to cool it.

Exit sign above door leading to porch and Palace Ave. Bright blue window frames across the street.

Phone rings and woman across from me answers her cell and talks as she eats, "Yes." She says and puts cell down.

"I know general manager of Monte Sagrado. I love what he said about the business here. They try to get groups in for weddings, conferences. They want to have something unusual. He comes up with good ideas. The theme events are wonderful. People from Philadelphia are looking for that. There's a lot of ranch property around here."

Woman finishes quiche busses her plate and leaves. Unusual to come here just to eat. It's a place people linger. Isn't that what drinking tea is about?

In rereading I see I slipped in my opinion here and there. The instruction was *No Interpretation. Just write what's in front of you.* What can I say? I have no defense.

So why don't you try this short practice? Be smarter than I was and appoint a more realistic time of day. It might be the cafeteria at work. Integrate it with what your life is. Every day, seven consecutive days, at your child's playground. The situations are endless. Remember: record what is in front of your face. Visually, aurally, how it feels. But also what is in front of your face is metaphorical. What is in front of your face could be a bounced check, your father dying, your son in the armed services overseas. But you must also not get lost with what you carry inside you. Include the woman across the room with the toddler, how he yanks at her scarf while she tries to sip coffee and speaks to the man with the Adam's apple sitting across. Let the concrete world anchor and ground you.

I had another idea. You might also choose a place in the woods. No human conversation but each day the same location could attune you to the natural environment—and you'd have to form language for what you do not know.

Or here's another angle of practice. Instead of words, John Daido Loori, Zen teacher and friend, told me he studied with Minor White, the great photographer, who had his students spend all afternoon searching outside for one spot that felt right to them, then sit and meditate there until that spot gave them permission to photograph it. Then they were to take a single shot. Very different from the constant snap snap snap of cell phones. Imagine the depth, the dropping through into attention. You and what you see, you and your surroundings are one.

Another practice I did in a café over ten years ago. Bread & Chocolate on Grand Avenue in St. Paul, Minnesota, to be precise.

For a full six months, two or three times a week, at different times of day, mostly mid-afternoon, when it was empty, with a single hot tea in a tall paper cup, holding it in front of me on the table, I just sat there for at least forty minutes. The tea disguised that I was simply doing café meditation, breathing in and out, practicing in society. When the time was up, I purchased a single hot chocolate chip cookie, fresh out of the oven, and ate it slowly, one nibble at a time.

Tremendous unemployment right now. Take advantage of this time you can't find work. Slice into your worry, time for practice. You might be able to look back on this period with gratitude.

This exercise of including your surroundings, even in a noisy café, does calm and ground the mind. In practice we should have no idea of gaining something. And yet, in doing this café practice you might receive at least—almost for sure—yourself. What's better than that. You are you. Nobody else. Not Queen Elizabeth, Keith Richards, or that young man who created Facebook. Not even Venus Williams or Madonna. That's how lucky you are.

Six-Word Memoir

How can we keep our practice from getting sleepy? I just heard from a student who has been working on a complicated book for the last several years, part biography of an artist, part memoir about herself. She's determined this year to near the end. Good aspiration but beware. Your writing can get tight, no air, no breath, no fun. (I notice I'm using the word *fun* lately connected to practice. Yes, fun in the best sense: a feeling of play, integration. The world settled in as it should be, all intact. Wholesome.)

She said she feels like she's slugging through right now. This is the signal to take a new approach—or at least relax.

For me, I sometimes let something in my immediate presence inform me, say a chicken sandwich (feeds me, too) or a glass of water on my desk or a book I grab off my shelf: *Not Quite What I Was Planning: Six-Word Memoirs,* collected from *Smith* magazine, near at hand. Yes, the title tells you everything of what to do.

I used the idea to freshen a slump in an October afternoon. A Wednesday, the second full day, when students were settled enough to hear their critic's voice exclaiming, *What are you doing here?* after the exhilaration and expectation of traveling a long way to Taos for a retreat. "Let's do some six-word memoirs." Heads snapped back as though I'd splashed them with ice water. "You have five minutes. Don't think. Write several. Then see which one you like best."

Here are some they wrote:

> My singing voice was never heard
>
> Sorta kinda wanna whata wobbly wow

Fixer upper: don't inspect too closely

You can't take me with you

24 addresses but still no home

Brooklyn girl makes good: parents dumbfounded

Dear Abby, free advice, unsolicited usually

Car for sale no wheels included

Walking time bomb needs handsome detonator

Is this boat sailing to somewhere?

Spiritual one in family of mathematicians

Barbed wire pricked my American blood

His round ass makes me salivate

The child looked up and screamed

So long, thanks for the attention

Half a memoir: oh poor me

You're pretty in your own way

Lie to father, now to self

Why do newspapers have to die?

Bitch, Benefactor, Racist, Homophobe, Beauty: Mother

Laziness or fatigue: Does it Matter?

Married a rabbi; still a feminist

Money was the currency of control

Once handicapped now disabled still human

Walks and talks like real person

Cross eyed, pigeon toed, smart though

Cats dogs lovers kids more dogs

I am always changing my mind

Grandmother, no education; granddaughter, no limits

Sometimes we use too many words, too much effort. It con-fuses us, masks what we truly want to say. Now, Saundra, go back to your book in progress. Can a chapter be lively chunks you put together? Can you write from a whole fresh angle and a new kind of effort?

Age

There are years that ask the question and years that answer.
—ZORA NEALE HURSTON

In the most recent yearlong intensive at least five women were in their seventies. We all have ideas about what it is to be seventy, seventy-three, seventy-seven but, in truth, we have no idea. It's the job of these women to tell us. Each one will have a different experience. And we need to listen. If we are lucky, one day we will get there.

On the first morning, one seventy-eight-year-old pulled her hip out bending over to put on her shoe. The ambulance came and by evening after a hard yank by a doctor standing over her, she was back in her room. It was quite an ordeal. I thought for sure she would go home, but when I visited her she was raring to go.

"I'm not missing class," she said fiercely, pen and notebook in hand.

I watched her totter and scramble over the icy below-zero terrain. She was on time for every session.

A young woman of twenty-eight is in the class. She works with computers in Silicon Valley. I was twenty-eight once but I had a different life. Computers didn't exist then. We need her to tell us what it is like to be her age in 2011.

Another woman just became forty and lives in Brooklyn. One is fifty and has a nine-year-old daughter and lives in Austin, Texas. One is sixty-four married to a doctor in Atlanta and one is forty-seven, living in Athens, Georgia, and one is sixty-two from Miami and one is fifty-eight from a small town in Mexico.

The point is age is different for everyone. My forty-five was different from yours. No two people's lives when you get down to the intimate details are alike. Think of all the people in your town, then state, country. Then country to country. We assume too much: They are French, they are Chinese, and we leave it at that. Wonder of wonder of wonder. Don't assume anything. Pay attention. Look, listen.

Share your story. But not your story in a rote, for-the-hundredth-time sort of way. Settle down inside yourself and give it to us like you never heard it before, as discovery.

Then imagine your story is over. You threw it in the pile. And your parents' story is gone. Finished. *Quickly, quickly, without thinking, before your parents were born what was your original face?*

In a silent retreat when I tell my students to shut up (sometimes I try to be more polite), I cajole them that behind our words are no words. We have to know about silence.

And in meditation behind movement is stillness. We should know about that, too.

And behind our stories are no stories. How do we find out about that? What is our original face before we were created and rolled out our own set of trouble into the world?

I have a longtime friend who might and might not be dying of heart disease. He is walking the edge of life and death. In one hand is form and in the other, the void. At the back of life is death. But death would not exist without life. Help me with this. What can I tell him as he walks that sharp spine?

There is this and there is that. Can we write on moving sand? Can we stand on an ocean wave? How old are we anyway? Tell me.

Another seventy-year-old—seventy-three to be exact—in the middle of the week had a frighteningly fast-beating heart on the top of a flu.

"Where's the hospital?" her friend asked as she lunged into the reception room at ten in the evening.

Luckily, I was sitting there, too tired to get up and walk to the far building where I stay, so I was in a daze in a green chair, paging through a book on hikes in the Taos area.

My head jerked up. How could I explain directions in this dark mountain town, the turns and poorly lit street names, which at that flash moment, I didn't remember. "Follow me. I'll get my car."

And we drove too quickly on the long roads to the emergency entrance and tumbled into the waiting room.

"Forget the details," I yelled at the receptionist behind the window. "She needs help." The receptionist wanted birth date, insurance, address, next of kin. Logical things.

"Natalie, just settle down." She went back to her computer keys.

Oh, I forgot, I lived here for twenty years. She knew me. I became quiet and let the procedure roll on.

The student, Ren, ended up being in the hospital for four nights. Her heart was okay but she was running a high fever and they couldn't figure out why. The retreat was over on a Saturday at noon and on that Sunday she was let out. Her friend drove her down to a hotel in Santa Fe where she had been planning to look at art. Her daughter from Denver flew down to care for her and when she was stronger they were going to fly together to California, where she lived.

Ren is a longtime student of mine. The night before they left I invited her and her daughter over for dinner. I'd never met this daughter but I knew she had been in and out of drug treatment centers for years and now at almost fifty Elizabeth had been drug-free for a year and a half and some corner seemed to have been turned. The delightful thing was that the three of us were able to openly talk about it over the rice I overcooked, but the white fish and kale were good. A freedom pervaded the evening and the next morning when Ren called to thank me, I said, "You have till noon before you leave for your plane. What if I run over, pick you up, and take you to the Box Gallery, where I've been contemplating ocean paintings."

When I arrived, Elizabeth asked if she could come along and jumped in the backseat. At the gallery, Elizabeth immediately spied four small ocean paintings with moody skies and rough water. I had overlooked them, but she was right. They were the best. I thought, *I'll come back tomorrow and buy them,* but Elizabeth snapped them up just then. "They will inspire me to move to California near my mom."

I was spun around, then realized I wouldn't have seen them but for her pointing them out and she just saved me money. Then I stopped rationalizing and enjoyed her joy. When I dropped them back at the hotel, we stood in the parking lot, all three of us glowing. I looked over at Ren—for so many years she had worked to detach from her daughter's addiction—and now she was basking in their connection. I'd never seen her so happy.

As I drove away, I thought this was the completion of the retreat for her. We have ideas how a week we sign up for is supposed to go. But we don't know where it will take us. And if we only think, I missed class, I had the flu, I was in the hospital, we miss the fullness of our experience. Sometimes we are brought outside the schedule—and our plans. I remember being on a hundred-day retreat at a monastery and a woman became ill the first week and was pretty much bedridden for the full three months. Yet in the end she understood that this was her retreat and she seemed deeply satisfied as we packed to leave.

The world is big. Human beings, if we are fortunate, get to live a lot of years. No one can tell us how those years will go or give us a prescription for any decade. At twenty I thought you had to be successful at thirty or forget it. At thirty I surmised forty was the time. I also thought love came only in your twenties, that at sixty you were too old. All my thoughts were proven wrong.

A Third Thing

O ften we are caught between two things. Should I do this—or should I do that? A choice between two things is not a choice. It becomes a fight between right or wrong. A polarity is created and we are stuck. Usually neither one is good or bad, but we polarize them because of our pain in not being able to make a definite choice. *This one forever,* we want to say and be done with it. But then a nagging voice inside says, *No, not that one.* And we are pulled into the fray again.

This contention can go on for years.

We need a third thing, a way to step out of the conundrum. We don't realize it, but this third thing is fertilized and fueled by the energy of the other two. So don't despair. It is by taking on the struggle that something new can come out of it. It is our human effort and yearning, our care, that made us enter the struggle to begin with. Be careful not to lay an idea of goodness over your struggle. Keep it alive and raw.

The third thing that will arise is unique, individual—and real. It has to be, because it will change something for you from the roots up.

And don't be glib and now label everything the third thing. That's what my students did at first when I told them about this. "Yeah, yeah, I know. I'm looking for the third thing."

Leave a little space, an opening for something fresh to arise. It usually doesn't happen overnight. We have to be aware—and wait, holding the skirmish in our arms. This is where we build up our mettle not to act too soon. Let it all compost. The threads of our conflict are knitting something below the surface even as we wait for a resolution. Be patient.

In an early June meeting of a yearlong intensive retreat at Mabel

Dodge—the spring winds still ferociously batting around the branches of cottonwoods along the Taos ditches—we went around the room, each student naming an essential conflict they lived with. All sounded familiar, rang true. Two particularly pierced my heart: One woman, Judy, said she is an expert financial adviser and has been successful helping many families sort out and organize very complicated financial arrangements—she'd done this for over thirty years. She was well-known in her field. At the same time, her own personal family finances were in a shambles and she couldn't pull them together. She experienced a lot of shame around this disparity.

The other woman was young, had emigrated to the United States from a country full of injustice and extreme oppression. She was actively involved in radical social politics and her conflict was between being sympathetic toward armed revolution in countries all over the world and the open love she felt when practicing Zen.

I looked at her and said, "A third thing might be a real relief."

She half smiled but her mouth didn't curve up.

I had no answers for them, no magic third thing that would wrap up and put a bow on their conflicts. "Let's write for ten minutes, exploring your opposing contentions even further. Go to extremes if you like to help find some middle." When we were done, I told them, "Now let's let it rest." I rang the bell three times and we sat for thirty minutes.

The students continued to practice: to write, to do individual sitting and walking at home between seasonal weeklong retreats.

Six months later, at our next retreat, Judy reported that she'd written an article in a local town newspaper about her family's financial shambles. She was tired of hiding, yet she was also terrified her clients would read it and fire her. Instead she said the paper received many positive letters in response, which they printed, saying how much they understood her problem and how brave she was to admit it, how they admired her honesty in these hard economic times. This encouraged her to write more articles and proclaim more about her financial straits. She was radiant as she sat in the corner of the zendo, telling this.

I said, "Judy, that's your third thing—to enter the fear." Her third thing was the action she took—and it was through writing. Maybe as the writing teacher, I couldn't see it, because it was so obvious.

I first met Dorotea at a retreat at the Zen Mountain Monastery in the Catskills right after 9/11. She'd taken a train up from her home in Brooklyn and couldn't stop crying in class. I never asked her why. For the pain and suffering in New York, for finding a place of refuge and relief at the monastery? Ever since then she'd been studying with me.

In the last session of the intensive ten years after 9/11, on a Friday afternoon in November as we were in the process of breaking silence for the week, she declared that during afternoon break, in this very zendo, she had written the last words of the first draft of her novel.

"Whoa, we never knew you were even writing a novel. We have some questions for you," I said. "What's it about?"

She waved her hand. "A beauty queen everyone adores in the Philippines who becomes a symbol of freedom."

"What's the structure of the book?" I asked, testing her.

Her eyes lit at the question. "When I read Faulkner's *As I Lay Dying,* I knew I had the right structure."

Her novel, which we found out she'd been writing for several years, worked the polarities of her conflict into a creative third action. Writing can be revolutionary. Dorotea was actively working on the third thing all along. This time, too, writing was the resolution.

When we first went around the classroom back in June, declaring the conflicts we live with, I told the group mine: I'm torn between my love of Taos and my love of Minneapolis and they are both such opposite places. When we wrote afterward, I realized that Taos, in its wildness, in its mountains, dirt roads, cragged adobe houses (I even lived in a teepee for a while), allowed me to have deep awakening experiences. The land echoed and supported what was happening inside.

Then in living in the Midwest and meeting Katagiri Roshi, I found the language and structure to root those awakenings in order to pass them on. And I found that not only in the zendo there but even in the orderly organization of streets and blocks, sidewalks and individual square lawns, Minneapolis fed my understanding of structure.

The third thing, Santa Fe, the place I've lived now for six years, often questioning why I was there, was actually the resolution of Taos and Minneapolis. It had mountains and it also had ordinances. And I wasn't so passionate about Santa Fe as I was about Taos and Minneapolis, so I had even more peace there.

The retreat ended on a Saturday, and on Sunday, back in Santa Fe, I walked past an open-house sign. I went to the front door—oh, it was too modern for me, I already knew I didn't like it—but then I thought sometimes they serve fresh baked chocolate chip cookies to lure customers. I stepped in, looked down the hall, and went immediately over to the owner and made a bid. I knew it was my house.

Understand, I was not impulsive. I'd lived off solar energy—all my electricity and heat was from the sun—for twenty years in Taos. Whenever during the six years I lived in Santa Fe and looked at houses, they felt like gas guzzlers, not built to take advantage of the abundant New Mexico sun. But in "browsing" houses over those years, I developed a compass for what I clearly wanted. This modern house had light, faced south, had cement floors to absorb the sun's rays, had compost bins out back, was walking distance to town and across the road from the Zen Center. I could hear the wooden thump of the han in the morning, calling students to zazen.

By evening I had signed a contract. This time a *house* in a third town was the third thing. But do you see? The third thing is not a quick result. It evolved over a long time, developing while I was not conscious it was happening.

The awareness of the possibility of a third thing is important. It allows us to get unstuck, to take a backward step, a breath, a different perspective. Otherwise, tired of the conflict, we grab one half or the other and, as many of us have found out, it can be disastrous.

Moshe Feldenkrais, a physicist, a black belt in judo, who created a remarkable method of body integration and movement, was living in Russia at a time of constant large and small raging wars. Great suffering was everywhere he looked. As a young boy he thought he could join the army and maybe help that way—or work to try to resolve things through politics. But he said to himself, *Two things are not a choice.* At fourteen (you grow up fast in areas of great conflict) he discovered his third thing: he left Russia, walking for six months across Europe to Palestine. So did that resolve everything for young Moshe? For a Jewish boy in the early 1940s, the idea of Israel afforded hope and great possibility.

We should remember human life is constantly crossed with the dark and the light. We are deluded to think we can find a solid island of safety and forever hold on tight. That's what gets us into trouble in the first place. We grab one thing and go blind—or fight between two, thinking one will win.

What deep conflict haunts you? Where are you pulled in two different directions? Where are you wrestling to no avail?

Write about the polarities without trying to come to a conclusion.

Take a slow walk down your street. Let the details of the light, trees, buildings fill you. Let the world come home to you. Plant the conflict deep in your belly and be nurtured with what's around you.

Sit and feel the goodness of being a human being. This conflict is the ground to step forward into the present moment. If it's hot, let it be hot. Don't run for an air-conditioned room. Let what is, be what is. Something new will be born.

Cynicism

I'm lost on a hiking trail in Colorado, it's about to pour, and my mind wanders to planning a day workshop of walking and writing with Katie Arnold, who is just forty and as fit as a nail. Not one drop of body fat, she hauls her one-year-old weighing eighteen pounds in a pack on her back up fourteen-thousand-foot mountains, while her husband carries the older daughter, weighing thirty pounds. I don't intend our day workshop to be anything that vigorous, maybe a soft hill, through a meadow a few miles outside of Santa Fe. Hey, maybe Diablo Canyon, west of the city. Lots of drama, intense beauty, but not much heft.

I'm getting really lost now—in my mind and on the trail. Rivulets of water are running down the wet path. I didn't bring a rain poncho but I don't care. It's only water and I can see the town of Ouray way below. Eventually I'll find my way. So I'm thinking about how Katie knows stuff about hiking I'll never know. (Yes, always bring a poncho, but she's not dogmatic and what I want to know is not about practical matters.) I hike with her every Tuesday morning we are both in town but I never ask her these questions, about what she knows. I'm building them up. I want to teach the students in our workshop to develop a curiosity, not a blunt acceptance—*Katie's a good hiker*—but a thirst for understanding, connecting links; creating wrinkles in the gray matter of our brains feeds a penchant to see below the surface. Otherwise, how can we write? Surfaces do not make the cut: *Katie's thin and led the walk. It was fun. Nature is nice to walk in.*

We want to ask Katie questions that make her think: What motivates you? Tell us about the first time the hunger for mountains awoke in you. Is this how you first connected with your husband? Were you afraid having children might hinder you?

Do I sound nosey? What can I tell you? Writers are nosey. How do things come together? What is the drive underneath?

Here's a good one: How come an athlete like you is willing to go every Tuesday morning with a dreamer like Natalie, huffing up the hill, twenty-three years older? Is that nasty? No. Writers tell it like it is.

Of course, I can speculate. Katie could be generous, for one. But sometimes it's good to not take anything for granted. Ask the question and listen to the answer.

And, please, don't forget to ask a few details about the environment. What's the name of that brush up ahead? That line of ragged rock? Want to know and take it in. In our society we often ask idle questions to fill space, expecting everything to be named and qualified. Most of all, pay attention. Deep attention.

And now here is the quandary, the pitfall of developing a writer's mind. The mind can become stuck, leaning toward the dark. It's good to be astute, discriminating. To not take things at surface value but to train ourselves to know things as they are, including the willingness to also see corruption, betrayal, greed, the world askew. Penetrating into situations can also develop cynicism. Even an innocent walk can turn into a diatribe. What are those sounds up ahead? Oh, no, dune buggies with three kids under ten, tearing up the environment. Why aren't they exercising their bodies? It can go on and on. Eventually, a writer can become an opinionated old grouch unable to bear humanity.

Bill Moyers was recently on National Public Radio speaking to this. He said that what keeps him from cynicism is an act of will, a decision to not fall on that side no matter what.

Developing a sitting practice also helps, creating space, a connection to the heart, a grounding in the wisdom of impermanence, egolessness, a coming back to zero. Otherwise, the world's troubles are hard to bear. We become numb, callous, or continually angry.

Philip Gourevitch, who wrote *We Wish to Inform You That Tomorrow We Will Be Killed with Our Families: Stories from Rwanda,* went back again and again to Rwanda to understand the dynamics of the massacre of Hutus by Tutsis and to precisely communicate those dynamics so we may understand. He continues to write articles illuminating Rwanda's progress into peace and its complications.

After I read his book, I spontaneously called the *Paris Review,* where he was an editor. I never expected to get through, but in a moment the receptionist connected us.

"Yes?" he said.

"I just read your book. Thank you for your effort."

Silence at the other end. I felt silly. "Well, that's all I called for."

We hung up.

I was unprepared. I should have asked him what keeps him going.

In the book he says his family were Holocaust survivors and he wanted to continue the vow of "never again." For horror not to repeat itself endlessly we have to understand its makeup, be willing to look at it, get close to it, at the same time not burn up with it.

What we avoid corrupts and deforms us—we are always twisting away from it. And it shows in our writing, in the way we sit and walk.

If it is true that we are interconnected, then, in avoiding something, we avoid ourselves. We say Africa is the dark continent. It's our own darkness we have projected on it. We have pillaged, colonized, raped it. And then we say it's their fault.

The students in the most recent yearlong True Secret Intensive at first balked at some of the reading assignments: *We Wish to Inform You That Tomorrow We Will Be Killed with Our Families, King Leopold's Ghost,* about the colonization and devastation of the Congo, an account of Japanese prisoner-of-war camps in World War II, a memoir of a Filipino man immigrating to California, two books on the Jewish Holocaust. But as we read and discussed them, the understanding became liberating, energizing. We became more alive. We no longer carried our fear in our unconscious; it came forward, in front of us, where we could see and claim it.

Simone de Beauvoir wrote in *The Second Sex* that, in order to create, we must be deeply rooted, not living on the periphery, the position of most women in our society. The vibrancy comes from moving right into the center, being alive to what is truly happening.

In meditation sit with what you fear till you digest it, know it, it is no longer shut off from you, and your heart of love can open. It's not an easy process but it's a good process. We are not separate. The Greek economy falters across the big ocean and our economy here in the United States is shaken. Injustice and torture in Somalia or the Congo diminishes all humanity. After a killing on our own city block, fear ripples up and down the street—as does shame; we can no longer look our neighbors straight in the eye.

This is true. We all know it.

Bernie Glassman, a Zen teacher, has a practice called "Bearing Witness." You go into a hard, complex situation with the mind of not knowing, of having no idea or opinion, and, instead, feel, listen, and be in the actual situation, becoming one with it. This nonjudgmental state of mind can position you so that you might be able to find a way to help, not out of your own need to make something better so that you feel better or in order to alleviate your own fear, but so that you act when empty of yourself. You get yourself out of the way.

Glassman has brought people on five-day meditation retreats to Auschwitz, Rwanda, to live on the streets in New York, and into prisons. He realized that places of great suffering are also places of great healing but only if we first bear witness to the suffering there.

Often, caregivers, peace activists, writers, you name it, begin work out of deep concern but find that their concern turns into indifference because they cannot bear the pain. Sometimes we act as though we have found equanimity in our hard work, but we may be disguising our aversion or numbness because we can't take it anymore. Even our self-hatred can be a defense from feeling things as they are. We need to learn compassion not only for those we work with but also for ourselves. This spiritual component can sustain our work.

During times of stress and disconnection, I have found it helpful to repeat this loving kindness practice:

> *May I be happy*
> *May I be peaceful*
> *May I be free*
> *May I have the ease of well-being*
> *May I be safe*
> *May I be healthy*

In traditional practice you then expand it to others and the world, but I have found that if I can drop down to feeling it emanate in myself, it naturally expands out to everyone and everything else. And you can shorten it. Whisper: happy, peaceful, free, ease, safe, healthy. No subject, no object, no giver, no receiver.

Letting Go

It is the last morning of a full week of a True Secret silent retreat and we are very quiet.

Usually I encourage the students to anchor their minds in their breath when we are sitting. "Whatever you are thinking, wherever your mind takes you, cut through, back to the breath."

All week of this retreat I have explained that it is okay that the mind wanders. It is normal, but the practice is to keep coming back, to not believe every thought, and to not let those thoughts take you down the mind road away from here. The act of returning to the breath, to the present moment, each time is what strengthens the mind and gives it muscle.

But this last morning, it feels that we've settled so deep, that we are resting in the breath like a luxurious couch. Cry of magpie, car engine, dog bark, sudden soft light along wood floor as sun breaks through cloud outside, we even feel the bare cottonwoods scratching the sky. Of course, the cottonwoods aren't in the room but we are sitting with everything now. In the center of it all.

I whisper, "Let go," no other instruction, and it feels as though the room has fallen through to the bottom, the bottom of the mind.

But what does it mean to "let go"? I interrupt the group while we are silently sitting: "Okay, let's stop for a moment. Take out your notebooks. List all the elements a human being has to let go of in order to be present right here. For instance, your identity—country, age, gender."

They were momentarily shocked that I spoke an assignment into the silence without first ringing the bell twice to indicate the end of sitting. I was surprised, too, but off we went into our notebooks. Then we went around reading from our list.

race

religion

state

occupation

wanting things to be different

history

culture

waiting

being successful

being right

being a good or bad writer

money

irritation

what to keep, what not to keep

hunger

hope

effort

need

attachment

leaving

death

appearance

After one round it felt that we must have listed everything and we were all amazed when we went around again, how much more there was.

earnestness

lust

regret

envy

resistance

excitement

time

concepts

expectations

betrayal

group dynamics

obsessions

whether I have enough

judgment

belief

status

disappointment

duality

fear

relationships

straight spine in sitting

"Let's sit again. Can we drop all this burden?" I rang the bell three times, hoping to separate our astonished excitement from this new moment of sitting.

It was hard to get back to that deep quiet place. We were hyped up: opinion, we hadn't mentioned "opinion." What felt vast this time was not the open emptiness, but the awe at all the constructions we build and back ourselves into, all the constrictions we create to form ourselves. Even our names. Not that we should all be unformed, no moniker, coming from no place, going no place, but isn't that the real truth of our existence? Who are we anyway? *I come from the United States.* What does that really mean? From all fifty states?

We are talking here about freedom. We can't run from our identities, but maybe we can wear them a little lighter, not so heavy.

And when we sit down, trying to let go, we can breathe down through all these strictures and fill our bellies. Think about it: when we close our eyes and take a breath, do we have a B.A. from college?

The world had been so luminous the week of retreat, the beginnings of winter so alive out the door, so alive in us, too, the short days, the long darkness, the dry low rustle of weeds, the cold on our face, the tingle in our nose, the smell of piñon fires. I rang the bell after twenty minutes. "Should winter be on the list—a thing to let go of?"

Maybe the idea of winter, we decided, but not the true experience of it.

Then we moved into slow walking around the room, one foot after the other, then outside barefoot on the cold slate porch and down the sun-warmed wood ramp onto the open courtyard, light and cold pouring over us.

"Standing still," I barked.

We all put our two feet together, arms at our sides. So rarely do we let ourselves just stand.

After three breaths we stepped with our left foot and continued slow walking into the room again and back to our places.

I threw out: "Okay, now let's get personal and particular. What do *you* have to let go of? Go. Ten minutes. See what comes up."

> I have to let go of cinnamon, curry, paprika, melatonin, blueberries, the ocean, the memory of my father in navy blue swim shorts, the imprint of feet in the sand, the smell of Coppertone, chicken sandwiches in waxed paper, bending my head back with a bottle of Pepsi around my lips, a chipped white painted building with a screened porch, long shadows in the afternoon and wet hair clinging to my forehead. The taste of jam. Blackberry

vines, a dog named Fluffy. Salami sandwiches on white bread with a smear of mustard, lace curtains, my grandfather with his shirt off mowing the lawn. I'd have to let go of the old past of lilac bushes, Oak Neck Lane, cement steps, cracks in sidewalk, lawn chairs, green garage, a driveway, a block, a hill, pavement, curb, a patch of weeds, the yellow air, a pistachio shell caught between my teeth, my Aunt Lil, Cousin Juney, Kenny, Aunt Rae and Uncle Sam. Hoping to get home before dark, a lucky penny in my grandfather's drawer and my grandmother in her pink plaid dress and thick shoes.

We had not mentioned letting go of memories. Even sweet ones. Not because they are bad but when sitting, we sit. Not wander off to Louisiana, to summer, to a cool drink. Save that for writing. And save yourself for the grit and wonder of the present moment—don't miss it.

So, now, darling reader, forget the list we made here on a December morning. Sit down and make your own list of the constructs that you shoulder unconsciously, the stances that were bred into you, the true and the false. Don't worry that you might repeat some already listed. If they come to your mind, I am afraid they are yours.

Now sit in a sunny place or a warm place or under a tree—or sink into the place where you are. Take a deep breath and fall down through it all to just being. Let go. Enjoy yourself. Hopefully, right now you are feeling too amiable to get personal.

At another time—later in the day, this evening, tomorrow, maybe a week from now—go to a different level, get personal, get down, not a list, but writing practice, keep your hand going—what can you let go of, what do you carry? Twenty minutes. Be honest. Follow the odd thought, twisted memory, peripheral intuition, or distant color that comes up as you write. This leads to a closer scouring of the mind.

Look over your shoulder. There's nothing there. We carry it all inside us.

◆ ◆ ◆

PART FOUR

Encounters and Teachers

I vow to wake the beings of this world

I vow to set endless heartache to rest

I vow to walk through every wisdom gate

I vow to live the Great Writer's Way

—slightly altered Four Boundless Vows,
original translation by Joan Sutherland and John Tarrant

Teachers

Dear reader, do you know Issa? The great Japanese haiku writer? His mother died when he was two. At six he wrote his first poem:

> Oh, motherless sparrows
> Come,
> play with me

What do you hear in this poem? Raise your hands—

> compassion, yes
>
> sorrow, yes
>
> playfulness, yes

What else?

> loneliness, yes
>
> emptiness, yes
>
> wanting connection, yes
>
> kindness, yes

This kind of poem helps both teacher and student expand our vision.

About twenty-seven years ago, twenty writing students from Santa Fe flew to Minneapolis to study with me at a monastery, several hours' drive south of the city. One tough, inquisitive, punchy student had the foresight to call ahead and arrange an interview with Katagiri Roshi, who was still alive, and whom she could see before we drove down.

A day later I asked her, "So what happened?"

"Not much," she answered with a shrug of her shoulders. "I came in and asked him, 'What's Zen?'

"He was sitting cross-legged under a low table in his study. He picked up a book. 'You can either drop the book like this . . . ' He carelessly dropped the book on the table." She motioned to show me with her hands. "'. . . or you can place it down like this.' He mindfully placed the book on the table. 'This second way is Zen.' Then he bowed and the interview was over." She shrugged again and the corners of her mouth went down.

Katagiri did not waste time. She either got it or she didn't.

Everyone wants a piece of a teacher but often we realize that piece only many years later. If we are lucky, some recognition finally comes to us. That simple practice, what Roshi once said was the goal of Zen, *to have kind consideration for all sentient beings every moment forever*—and by sentient beings he meant not just cats, dogs, and people, but the floor, ceiling, walls, shoe, tree, apple, cup, lamp—extended into all parts of our life.

Even my clothes: no matter how late at night it is or how tired I am, I simply cannot flop into bed without folding and putting them away—and I don't care that much about clothes. But my opinion doesn't matter. A student in an intensive made folding her clothes one of her designated practices, because usually she strew them all over the place. Liking, not liking, judging. *The Great Way is not difficult, just avoid picking and choosing* (Third Zen Ancestor, around A.D. 600). Practice bleeds through our life—and beyond our life. I imagine the folding continuing after I die. The folding of clothes will not be frozen or permanent but unbroken.

A student I knew ten years ago appeared again in the first row of another class. Of course, it is not exactly Michele but someone similar to her gestures, to the tilt of her head. We endure—and don't.

Can we walk that thin line between constant change and continuation? And in the middle of this flux, feel gratitude but not hold on? Gratitude greases the joints to let us let go, and at the same time to stop and realize we received something. Gratitude is the most developed and mature of human emotions.

To have a teacher is a fine thing. I feel sad when I hear teaching and school maligned. In the middle of the chaos of my childhood family, I learned order from roll call, desks in a row, squares of time called periods and bells ringing, signifying the end and beginning of periods. Not so different from Zen protocol. Many people go to the military to learn this.

In ancient China, a teacher was honored above all else. When the merchant class developed, even with their wealth, the common people were not impressed. But a teacher, poor, in rags, held a high position. True generosity and care lay within the teacher. This poor person dedicated his life to sharing and imparting knowledge, thus making a richer society.

A teacher taught us to read, write, and do math. To pick up an implement—pen, keyboard, pencil—and form letters, elementary skills but foundational. Thank you, Miss Miller, Miss McKee, Mrs. Schneider, Mrs. Post, Mr. Berke. Many elements contributed to where we are now.

In sixth grade Mr. Nolan stumbled over my schoolbag every single time he walked down the aisle where my desk was. In the single worn gray suit he wore every day, he never thought to tell me to move the bag and neither did I. Even now I can see his straight nose and straight dark hair, as he trips and catches himself and disturbs not my concentration, only my whispering with the girl next to me. What was her name? Short blond hair, no father, a single mother—Chris, that was it. Where is she now? Mr. Nolan, thank you. I don't remember what I learned but I was eleven, turning twelve, and you were with me. In another time and place I move the brown fake leather schoolbag so you may walk freely.

The Blazon

Miriam is in front of the blackboard at Santa Fe Community College teaching the class blazon, a French poetic form that lists the attributes of the beloved.

Leave it to the French. What could be more important?

The dean of the school pops his head in the class. "School is closed. Right now. The new governor has declared a state of emergency. Leave the building. The gas is being turned off to conserve energy."

Twenty-two below, thirty below. My friends in Minnesota, North Dakota are laughing at us. What wimps. A few days of real cold and the state collapses. What if it were a war? We are not equipped.

Miriam's students dash for the door. She is left at the blackboard. "But, but," she incants, "I'm teaching a very important form of poetry. About love. What is more important? Love will keep you warm." She is talking to their backs. "Stop now. Stop. Class, where are you going?" But they are gone.

In defiance I bundle up and go for a hike. With so many layers of clothes and my heart pumping as I climb altitude, I am boiling and have to take off my hat and gloves. But New Mexico is a poor state and not everyone has layers of clothes.

As I drive home listening to the news, I think, *I don't care what anyone says*. I'm certain literature is the most important thing. Where would we be without our writers, even the ones I have never read? My friends and I did not choose something peripheral to dedicate our lives to. We are not irrelevant.

Go ahead, Miriam, tell me about the form.

The term *blazon* describes a genre of poetry, beginning in the sixteenth century, used to praise a woman by singling out different parts of her anatomy and creating appropriate analogies. It's been used in literature ever since. One famous example is by Shakespeare, who ironically rejected each common cliché:

> My mistress' eyes are nothing like the sun;
> Coral is far more red than her lips' red;
> If snow be white, why then her breasts are dun;
> If hairs be wires, black wires grow on her head.
> I have seen roses damasked, red and white,
> But no such roses see I in her cheeks,
> And in some perfumes is there more delight
> Than in the breath that from my mistress reeks.
> I love to hear her speak, yet well I know,
> That music hath a far more pleasing sound.
> I grant I never saw a goddess go;
> My mistress when she walks treads on the ground.
> And yet, by heaven, I think my love as rare
> As any she belied with false compare.

You have to love Shakespeare. He's cut through and brought love down to earth. He takes a stock metaphor and says no. It's his own version of waking up.

Here are a few lines from André Breton's blazon, "Free Union," where he walks the edge into a list poem but that is fun, too:

> My wife whose hair is a brush fire
> Whose thoughts are summer lightning
> Whose waist is an hourglass
> Whose waist is the waist of an otter caught in the teeth of a tiger
> Whose mouth is a bright cockade with the fragrance of a star of
> the first magnitude
> Whose teeth leave prints like the tracks of white mice over snow
> Whose tongue is made out of amber and polished glass

Whose tongue is a stabbed wafer
The tongue of a doll with eyes that open and shut
Whose tongue is an incredible stone

—Translated by David Antin

The poem fits its title, "Free Union," which gives us permission to associate wildly and trust the flash glances from the periphery of our minds. This is good. It widens and empties us. Then when we sit in meditation after we write, we can be quiet.

Try writing a list blazon, quickly, without thinking. Let's bring everyone back into the classroom for Miriam. This exercise loosens the muscles, aims for the ridiculous, is nonlogical. *She's bigger than a horse and wider than a mountain. Come to me, my tiny mouse, pebble on the beach, apple in a lost eye . . .*

And don't forget that in some parts of the world, such as Asia, sentient beings include not just human beings or chickens. Even a chair, a doorpost, a marble is considered alive. How about a blazon to a book or a front step?

Let's remain in Miriam's class as the radiator peters out. Let's have her read to us her modern list blazon from her book, *The Widow's Coat*, which she wrote in 1999 to her husband who died too young:

My husband in stubble, zen priest in a nicotine patch
My husband by the open grave with a handful of dirt
My husband the Jew, bleeding from ulcers
My husband in ivory beads carved into skulls
A man with designer sunglasses, speeding tickets,
    the collected works of Han Shan
Of weight loss, skinny as Auschwitz, whose new name is colitis
Whose other name means water course in Japanese
Whose name was taken from the western sycamore tree

Whose original name was changed on Ellis Island
Who began to vomit the day I kissed him
My husband who buys one pair of boots per lifetime
Who loses forty pounds, whose wrists
Make me hysterical, who molts, parakeet or polar bear
My husband who swam without his glasses
Towards a horizon marked by a red tanker
Who stood up and hemorrhaged rust
Who wrote his initials in blood
Who coached me in childbirth
Who owed me fifty dollars
Who gave me a mushroom
Who moves the sprinklers
Who cut up the counter with a carving knife
Who crossed his legs and sat down
Whose name was raven and anemia and something else secret
An internal organ shaped like Minnesota
Shadow, skeleton, moth owl
Sitting on a cache of eggs in the dark
City sitting on its own skyline
Empire State Building, Arc de Triomphe, Coit Tower
This curve of the world lit up by expensive
Electricity I call husband.

Now stop your twitting, tweeting, tottering, tumbling about the cold and write a blazon. You don't have a lover right now? Don't be ridiculous. They are all over the place. Turn your head—what about that young man in a heavy jacket, standing on the corner waiting for the light to turn. Write about him.

Or the old woman nibbling her sandwich, sitting on the sidewalk, leaning against the building's foundation, a grocery cart filled with plastic bags, hooked in front with her boot so no one will take it. Is she not our beloved? I am not being romantic here.

Your noticing, your listing her attributes is what sustains her, connects us to the force underneath no matter what the conditions. Forget for a moment about politics, the battle of wills, the transfer of power. Forget about manufacturing, shopping, money, the stock exchange, horse racing, airplanes, the science of our brains and technology. What is that force that drives us, that connection, that not being alone anymore? The great ground of being opens up and holds us. Sitting still joins us to that true marriage. Literature points the way.

But great literature is about great suffering, you say.

Isn't that the cornerstone? To suffer the world. To be here.

Go ahead. Write. Do as Miriam tells you. A blazon list. Right now. Go. I will give you ten minutes.

Okay, wind down. I'm calling time.

Now ten more minutes: list twenty things you cannot live without. Be honest. Your cell phone might be number one. Keep listing.

What would I write—without much contemplation, off the top of my head?

1. toilets

2. the skin and body of another human

3. water

4. chocolate

Before I go further I want to edit and evaluate. I scream in my head: *You are so superficial.* And then I tell myself, *Shut up and continue.* There is also curiosity, what does my niggardly mind come up with.

5. New Mexico

6. New York

7. my house

8. hot tea

9. paintings on the wall

10. my friends

11. the alphabet

I keep wanting to write "horses." I don't ride; I never owned one. But trust yourself. List it.

12. horses

13. bookstores

14. cafés and restaurants

15. Jewish food—blintzes, chicken soup, corned beef sandwiches on rye

16. the Atlantic Ocean

17. my interior life

18. hiking

19. yoga

20. trees

Is this a true list? Probably not. What is true? Maybe tomorrow I can sift down closer. What is essential? This is a practitioner's life. Not to act and react, but to notice, to come close to ourselves—and others—close to all things. Also accept our mind where it is and meet it there. Oh, Natalie, after all your organic eating you are still stuck on the Jewish deli where the only vegetable is a pickle?

Of course I am—and I'd like mustard on the rye.

What is it to be a human being?

I said to Miriam over dinner the other night, have you noticed that all our friends that we met twenty-five years ago are pretty much the same? Some may be more successful, a few have children, divorced, married again, but not that different. Changed but not changed.

I've also noticed that no matter how much my outward life seems to improve—a new house, a new girlfriend, a new book contract—I still have the same amount of inner torture, the same twisted agonies. Noticing this has helped. I recognize those old friends and don't believe them as much.

Let go, I whisper to myself.

And in retreat when we are sitting, I whisper it to my students again—and again, "Let go."

Wang Wei

Poetry, the One True Thing

As I walk in the evening to a poetry gathering, a loud crunch comes from under my boots on the five-day-old snow along the road's edge. I settle in a corner of a fat couch. Joan Halifax, holding in her hand a poem by Wang Wei, the eighth-century Chinese poet, translated by Kenneth Rexroth, begins: "When Rexroth was dying, Robert Bly took me to his bedside and I knew then he was a real poet."

She lifts the piece of paper with the poem on it, about to read further, when I jump in. "Wait, how did you know he was a real poet then?" I wasn't going to let her make that statement and not hear the rest.

Even though Joan carries all these jewels inside, sometimes it's someone else's inquisitiveness that brings them out. So here is your first poetic lesson: Don't be afraid to be hungry and want it all.

"Bly read Rexroth poems by Hafiz and Rumi while he quietly lay there with his eyes closed. It was as though those poets opened him so that, when Bly read Kenneth his own poems aloud, it was as if he were hearing them for the first time. Big tears rolled down his cheeks."

"Oh," I say and swallow.

Joan reads and Wang Wei's poem has the weight of a stone dropped directly into the human heart, rippling across centuries. All of us in the room feel it.

At twenty-four, poetry was my entry into the colored world of light and language. For thirteen years poetry filled me and then I wrote a prose book and never looked back. I abandoned a great love. Unintentionally. Something else glittered and I followed. The poets I knew then—Gerald Stern, Yehuda Amichai, Pablo Neruda, Linda Gregg, Sharon Olds—were the last poets I read. Great Western poets. Sophisticated, crafted.

But as I tell of this Chinese poet, I tremble. Wei's work is so simple you can almost miss it.

LILY MAGNOLIA ENCLOSURE

The autumn hill gathers the remaining light
A flying bird chases its companion before it
The green color is momentarily bright
Sunset mist has no fixed place

Wang Wei lays down one image after another, not trying to be poetic. That would get in the way. The light on the hill; two birds in the sky; the color; and then he notices how the mist at sunset has no stationary place. One, two, three, four. No evaluation, no judgment. Just seeing with an even eye. Austere and naked. He is giving us the mind of meditation. Close, so close it touches us now, so many centuries later. Nothing added on, no trill of nervousness, no busy thought commenting. Meeting the thing itself. And out of that, an enormous truth "no fixed place." Where are we? Who are we?

In our society poetry may be the one true thing. You can't get rich as a poet. You can't make poems pay for your gas or electricity. Everything else in our society has a price. Poetry from the beginning is hopeless.

So poetry is a good practice. It can take us to the place where we might encounter the unknown that has always been known. The truth is you are no dummy. Take the cake out of your mouth, take off a few layers of makeup, wipe the sleep from your eyes. Do you see it? Here and here and here. I studied and sat intensely for many years, not in order to learn something new but to give form and structure to my own mind. Little Natalie in fourth grade—in second—smelled the wet bark in spring out the classroom window. But Mrs. Post and Miss McKee demanded that I look straight ahead at the blackboard. Meanwhile Robin Wagner in the seat in front of me was drawing her horse Peggy Sue in every margin of her notebook. Longing filled our room. Now the poet turns his head and nods, affirms who we are. Kenneth Rexroth meets himself at the edge of the great beyond.

Poetry takes time. If we give poetry a little time, it will give us something back. When I am impatient, I get nothing.

The Chinese during the Tang dynasty, that golden age from 618 to 907, wrote poems on many occasions, saying good-bye, setting off, on the way, to a cousin, to an official, inspired by a mountain.

Let's look at another poem by Wang Wei:

SEEING OFF YUAN THE SECOND ON A MISSION TO ANXI

> At Weicheng morning rain has dampened light dust.
> By the hostel, the willows are all fresh and green.
> I urge my friend to drink a last cup of wine;
> West of Yang Pass, there will be no friends.

The title not only affirms this poem-on-occasion tradition but tells of a specific juncture—no abstract, vague reason to write a poem. A friend is leaving and that matters.

Friendship is one of China's oldest art forms and Wang Wei cultivates it. Friendship is how he survived during his exiles from court life, the early death of his wife, of his mother. It is his consolation during seclusions in the mountains and during intrigue, disgrace, dismissal in civic life.

These Chinese poems are often full of wine. They liked their drinking, their human connection and conviviality. And wouldn't you? The landscape is wide with long passages of meeting no one.

THE TRUE SECRET OF WRITING

"West of Yang Pass" you are on your own. Yang Pass is a real place and beyond, it is unpopulated—or only with strangers. No need to talk of the void, of death, to conjure it up. All kinds of death are around us—in this poem there is the place that is the end of friends.

Wang Wei had a position in the courts. It was expected at this time that civil servants write poems—and it was even better if they were good at it. Wei was drawn to urban politics and also to the spirit in nature. He would vacillate between the two, back and forth between worldly and ephemeral concerns. In the city he longed for mountains; in solitude he longed for companions. Sound familiar? This was Wei's personal drama. Instead of a weakness it revealed his depth and intensity and gave humanity to his poems.

Here is a poem that shows the personal heart of Wang Wei:

FOR ZU THE THIRD

Spider webs hang from the beams,
crickets sing near the porch stairs.

At year's end, a cold wind.
Friend, how are you?

My tall house is dead. No one here.
Impossible to tell the feeling when you are gone.

A deserted gate, still and closed for the day.
Only the dropping sun slants into autumn grass.

Do you have a new message for me?
A thousand rivers and summit passes block
my way to you.

After you left I journeyed to Ru Ying
and last year went back to my old mountain.

We've been friends for twenty years
but never have used our talents.

You're always poor and sickly.
I watch my pennies.

Though it's mid-autumn and we're still not in
our hermitage
we'll be there by late fall.

Our time together is not these few lost days
become years
but my missing you is forever.

Eight years ago a friend left a note on my porch: *This one reminds me of you, good luck in your new house.* Attached was a Wang Wei poem, given in the tradition of an occasion: my titanic move from Taos to Santa Fe.

LAZY ABOUT WRITING POEMS by Wang Wei

With time I become lazy about writing poems.
Now my only company is old age.
In an earlier life I was a poet, a mistake,
and my former body belonged to a painter.
I can't abandon habits of that life
and sometimes am recognized by people of this world.
My name and pen name speak my former being
but about all this my heart is ignorant.

I sat on that porch for six years listening to the mourning doves on the telephone wire, watching the robins splash in the birdbath. In dry summers, the rabbits and chipmunks, too, stood on their hind legs and sipped from the bath.

Sitting on that porch I didn't know if I was a woman or a man, black or brown or white, Jew or Buddhist. It was a good time with the light coming through the piñons, a time before my old landlady died too early at eighty-five. She had tickets already for the next summer opera.

Now, you. It should be enough to read poems or hear about Wang Wei—and it is enough—but excuse me, I'm an old taskmaster, a camp counselor, a teacher. You'll know Wang Wei better if you work at it, imprint it in your body.

So, first, make a list of occasions that you could write poems for. This list creates structure, and it also alerts you to continue looking for occasions.

Now, of course, write a few. Stay with your senses, with what is. Maybe settle down a bit first. Take a slow walk, pick up three stones you like as you go. Turn each one over in the palm of your hand. Okay, six lines, go.

In the next three months let's pay homage to Wang Wei, to that Chinese culture from so long ago that honors the moment and our friendships. And it wouldn't be honest if we didn't use the things and situations of our world. Don't get fancy. Wang Wei is curious about us. He has given us his world. Give him yours.

Here's one by the poet Jack Gilbert:

HOMAGE TO WANG WEI

An unfamiliar woman sleeps on the other side
of the bed. Her faint breathing is like a secret
alive inside her. They had known each other
three days in California four years ago. She was
engaged and got married afterwards. Now the winter
is taking down the last of the Massachusetts leaves.
The two o'clock Boston & Maine goes by,
calling out of the night like trombones rejoicing,
leaving him in the silence after. She cried yesterday

when they walked in the woods, but she didn't want
to talk about it. Her suffering will be explained,
but she will be unknown nevertheless. Whatever happens,
he will not find her. Despite the tumult and trespass
they might achieve in the wilderness of their bodies
and the voices of the heart clamoring, they will still
be a mystery each to the other, and to themselves.

Pretty good. Now see what you can do.

Hemingway

What Is Not Said

I went to Key West for the third time because a Chinese friend had never seen it and wanted to, but I went to the Hemingway House alone. My friend, Baksim, didn't want to ride a bike so I rented one for myself. It was the third time I'd gone to Hemingway's house.

The first was thirty years ago with Kate Green, when we were both young writers. We were hungry for any sign or encouragement to continue: we reserved two beds in a hostel on the Keys for three nights and slept in a dorm room of ten with rickety iron spring bunk beds. We both slept on the bottom across from each other and whispered late into the night how every two years we vowed to write a book. We tried to find Tennessee Williams's spot on the coast where it was rumored he'd visited. Hemingway's house took us over like a tidal wave, the yellow stucco, green wraparound porch on the second floor, the long pool his second wife, Pauline, had built while he was away for ten months covering the Spanish War and having an affair with Martha Gellhorn. This first time we visited, the place inflamed our ambition, that ache to be heard, to be really good, to dedicate ourselves to literature forever.

Fifteen years later, I went again, when my mother lived alone up near Palm Beach and I was putting off seeing her for a few days— our relationship was always difficult. I remember taking a speedboat to a distant beach and being in a gay bookstore. I know I visited Hemingway's house again, but have only a distant rote memory. The imminent visit to my mother hung over my head. In her late eighties, she'd made a rash decision to sell her house and move across the country to Los Angeles and had asked me to do all the packing. Her house had sold immediately to a virile Italian with a gold chain hanging on his exposed hairy chest, but then she'd chickened out and pleaded with the man to withdraw his down payment and "let an old lady live in peace." I would be heading into this embroilment. The literary world of Hemingway took a backseat.

So this third time, twenty-five years after the first, ten after the second, clobbered me unexpectedly, though at the end of January the house was jammed with tourists, snapping pictures non-stop with their cell phones, and the tour guide I managed to find seemed to think he was Hemingway with his own red face and yellow beard. Every once in a while he took a nip from a silver canister as homage to the great writer and often repeated the words *manic depression*. Hemingway fought mental illness all his life. Even his drinking took on a different slant—as self-medication. By my third visit I also knew a fine southern writer who fought those same demons, a real torment even with help from good doctors. And back in Hemingway's day they didn't have many remedies. I imagined the deep depression that could keep his mind in a cement basement with no windows. He walked every evening to Joe's Bar after waking at 6 A.M. and going immediately to his workroom, an attic studio in a converted carriage house with a guest room below. A modest space, it had big windows, a rug, a small wood table in the middle with his typewriter and notebook, walls lined with bookshelves and a few paintings.

It was that room on the tour that stopped time. A palpable presence of concentration could still be felt there. I easily could imagine him right there settled deep into a scene and pouring it onto the typewriter keys. I wasn't the only one who felt it. Several tourists behind me gasped and were actually quiet for a moment. The guide read off a list of books Hemingway had written there, during the twelve years he and Pauline raised their two sons: *Green Hills of Africa, The Fifth Column, Winner, Take Nothing, To Have and Have Not,* and one of my favorites, *Death in the Afternoon.*

In the afternoons Hemingway fished on his boat with a Cuban man he'd hired, who became a good friend and was probably the model of the old man in his famous book. After he left Pauline, he married Martha, moved to Cuba, and bought a house there, where he wrote *The Old Man and the Sea.* Within five years he and Martha, too, divorced, and he continued to live in Cuba in the winters with Mary, his fourth wife. In the summers they lived in Ketchum, Idaho.

During the Cuban Revolution in 1959, Castro confiscated Hemingway's house and boat. He became so depressed at this loss, he couldn't shake it and consented to have electric shock treatment, hoping that would help. Instead it ruined his memory. He had no past and couldn't write. Eventually, he killed himself. The guide said, like his father did. It ran in the family?

The Old Man and the Sea won the Pulitzer and weighed the scales in his favor for the Nobel Prize in 1954. He wrote the first draft of his acceptance speech on the back of a paperback and, I'm told by two students who saw the rough draft displayed at the New York Public Library in celebration of their hundredth year, the final version wasn't much different. The sentences were tentative, awkward, clumsy. You could feel his nervousness in what he wrote, which began, "Having no facility for . . ." Sharyn and Dorotea jokingly repeated these beginning lines often after they saw them, but underneath they were touched by his loneliness and insecurity. For so long he'd been put forth as the Great White Hunter, impenetrable and invulnerable. No writer, in truth, is like that. No human being, either.

After the tour I went back to the small bookstore behind the house. I bought the famous novella. I had loved it years ago, but having read so many books since, I'd forgotten this one. The first time I read *The Old Man and the Sea* was as an assignment in high school and though even back then it was undeniably good, the teacher alluded to the old man as a Christ—or religious—figure, which killed it for me.

I tucked the book in my purse and pumped my pink bike up and down the crowded Key West streets that were dripping with live oaks and blooming magnolias, until I met Baksim at noon at a house where we sat on the verandah.

"What is that?" She pointed at an old banyan tree extended across someone's front yard; the tendrils dropped along the branches had found wide root.

"In India whole families live in those trees," I said. It was a pretty wonderful tree for me, too, and I'd seen banyans many times. I tried to imagine what it was like for someone to see it for the first time.

From my purse, I took out Hemingway's book and opened to the dedication: *To Charlie Scribner and Max Perkins*. Scribner was a great publisher when Hemingway, Fitzgerald, Thomas Wolfe were alive. Max Perkins was their editor. The old-fashioned kind that used to tote a bag of groceries up long stairs to where you were writing and who lent you money and encouraged you. Perkins worked with Wolfe for months on his 1,114-page onionskin manuscript to cut it down and create *Look Homeward, Angel*. This publisher and this editor fostered American literature. Hemingway, bent over the page, was writing for nobody and everybody and I imagine also had in mind these two men who he knew would carry the book, if it was good enough, out to the public.

Baksim reached over, opened to the middle of the book, and read aloud. I was transported. Later I marked some of those paragraphs and, the next day, after we'd returned to Fort Myers on the ferry, we promised to read the whole book aloud to each other. As I drove through the flat land of Big Cypress and into the Everglades, I listened intently to Baksim read, as white egrets lifted off the river of swamp grass and we passed thatch-roofed enclaves of the Seminoles.

"I never thought I could be interested in a book about fishing," Baksim, who worked in information technology on Wall Street for thirty years, said, clutching the book, "but right now, it's all I care about."

Four weeks later, looking at my marked paragraphs, I wonder why I marked them. My life's been busy since that time in Florida and I need to settle to meet again the mind of the book. I open to page thirty-two and look again. "The sun rose thinly from the sea. . . ." I see it now. The word *thinly* makes all the difference, a specific sunrise and I'm there in the boat looking out. ". . . and the old man could see the other boats, low on the water and well in toward shore. . . ." I can see them, too. "Then the sun was brighter and the glare came on the water and then, as it rose clear, the flat sea sent it back at his eyes. . . ."

Hemingway cared about the sun and the gradation of light, not diminished but invigorated by the ordinary: a sunrise. And once you are there, the dream of the book unfolds page after page. And that old man becomes the best of men.

The book is only 127 pages. So much is said by so little being said. "If a writer of prose knows enough about what he is writing about he may omit things that he knows and the reader, if the writer is writing truly enough, will have a feeling of those things as strongly as though the writer had stated them" (from *Death in the Afternoon*).

What is not said is as important as what is said. The book creates room for us to be with the old man. And the book creates space inside us. We look up from the page and look around: The horizon is more vivid, the slow color of light, clouds, train tracks—wherever you are—bricks on a factory, bridge over river, woman in red hat scratching her nose, fog on window, black ice on street, cat dashes under fence—the world is ours.

There are many ways to meditate. Whatever opens us, softens the heart, makes us alive to this human world and helps us to bear it is our path.

Someday, I will visit Ketchum, Idaho, stand over Hemingway's grave, and say, Thank you, thank you, thank you.

◆　◆　◆

I assigned *The Old Man and the Sea* to the 2011 yearlong True Secret Intensive, which had had a tough beginning at the end of February. Temperatures had suddenly dropped to ten, twenty, and then twenty-five below. New Mexico had never seen temperatures this low and the Texas oil provider's pipes had blown. We were without heat for days. When I drove up from Santa Fe, where schools were closed, Mabel Dodge was like a meat locker. We met anyway, sitting in the zendo. I was the only one facing the window. The first morning I watched snow falling furiously over the sheets of ice already there on the walkway. Some of the students had come from North Carolina, Florida, Arkansas; many were from Texas and California. Their jackets, gloves, and boots weren't warm enough.

Amazingly, they returned for the second session in June. Then New Mexico was having a drought. One participant said, "My hair dries as I'm washing it." It hadn't rained in months and fires in Arizona hit the border. Smoke was in the air.

In September, I wouldn't have been surprised if there had been a locust plague.

On the second morning, I asked, "How many of you had read *The Old Man and the Sea* before?"

Almost all raised their hands. Mostly in school, they said. Jan spoke up: "Many years ago, I was taking an Evelyn Wood speed reading course and we had to read it in five, maybe ten minutes."

"I don't think a book like this could be written now," I said. Yes, other books will be written of our time but this old man was so close to the sea and to the fish he caught, no fishing pole or reel, the line wound around his hand, braced by his back.

Sonja, who lives in a small fishing village on the Mexican coast, said, "You wouldn't believe the equipment tourists bring with them now. They even have a device for locating the fish." We groaned and then no one said anything for a long moment, feeling instead inside the mystery of this book.

It was almost lunch. I broke the silence, giving them an assignment. *Write for ten minutes and like Hemingway use only one- or two-syllable words.*

I remember the day I stepped off the train in Rome in the summer of 1973. The train, long and dark green, with small, cloudy windows and steam hissing from the brakes and from a hole on top of the engine. The station, too, its high metal ribs arching over the row of platforms was from the past—a time I knew only from the stories of others. I stepped onto the platform, my suitcase in hand, and walked to the exit doors. I didn't know where I was going, but I knew American girls in Rome should be careful and look as if they knew their way. If they looked perplexed, Italian men would appear at their side to offer help. This was not to be accepted, though that is exactly what I did, but not yet. I walked through the huge grilled doors onto what turned out to be a side street. Taxis stood at the curb, but drivers stood about on the sidewalk, asking every one who passed if they needed a car. Coming from the Midwest, where all the streets run parallel to each other and where a line of taxis means you take the first one, I wanted to select the car or driver who had the right to be next. But there was no such thing. There was the loudest voice, the closest body (pressing against mine in a way that hinted at more than a ride), the most rapid waving hand—but nothing that I recognized.

—*Deborah Holloway*

The use of one-syllable words brings us closer to a thing. We have to give more detail to convey complex emotions and thoughts. A writer can't hide with big words whose ideas may be amorphous, blurry, or have other connotations for the reader. We have to search deeper in our hearts for the more intimate feeling that lies lurking under the big word. We can't stray as easily. Words like *fat, red, raw, dry, hot, old, long, dark* come closer to nailing an impression.

Now you try. Let Hemingway inform you. Remember: Good writers are ultimately our teachers.

Wendy

Hints of the South

Let's look at Wendy Johnson's writing. Longtime Zen practitioner, gardener, and author of *Gardening at the Dragon's Gate* (Bantam 2008). For the last sixteen years she has also written a quarterly column for *Tricycle* magazine on gardening. As she takes soil samples, we are taking writing samples from her August 2011 column:

> Just inland from the Pacific coast of Northern California, I stand hip-deep in the surge of summer. Padron peppers ripen, lime green and viridian, alongside plump opal eggplants overhung with the heat-bloated vines of Sun Gold tomatoes. Fat honeybees heavy with amber sunflower pollen shuttle through the slow loom of August. In this throb of fecundity, I long for the lean pulse of the arid Southwest.

No spare, black, white, straight-line Zen writing here. Summer is surging, eggplants are "opal"—and "plump"; the tomato vines, "heat-bloated"; honeybees, "fat," "heavy," "shuttle through the slow loom of August." This is luscious writing. You feel the weight of heat as you read. You're ready yourself to slather on Coppertone and lie down and roast brown in the exploding sun.

Later on in the article I extract another few sentences—we are studying writing here, not gardening:

No rain for 113 days; dark-blood and ash-gray skies acrid with smoke from wildland fires. I stood on the barren spine of the garden site with 25 Zen practitioners, neighbors, and friends, every moist molecule of ocean fog wicked out of me, plotting paradise at the fiery rim of the known gardening world.

Cool-tined digging forks entered the dry dust of Upaya soil and emerged, burning.

Now in full August this Zen garden is thriving, alive with spare yet muscular fertility. The dry mind of paradise drops down deep roots.

Wendy's writing is exactly how we think writing should be, the kind that creates envy—"I can't write like that." But this lush language comes naturally to her. Brought up all her life in the Northeast, when I first heard her writing over twenty years ago while I was doing a six-week practice period at Green Gulch Zen Farm I broke my silence: "Wendy, tell the truth. That's Southern writing. No one else can write like that."

She blushed and told the truth: "Well, my people are from Alabama."

"I thought so," I said and narrowed my eyes—I had been suspicious. Another Southerner embarrassed by her roots.

I've encountered it over and over, like the Germans' shame of the Holocaust. Slavery and the reluctance to give civil rights to African Americans creates a big scar in the historical psyche.

Wendy never lived in the South, though in her late teens she was on the Selma march, but the shame is passed on—as is the great heritage of language, appreciation of story, connection to the land, and knowledge of the particular, this flower, this tree, this bog, an honoring of their names. These are good ingredients for a writer—yes, even the guilt and the suffering. They push you on. The southerners lost the Civil War—they know failure. Fine writers have come from there—Richard Wright, Faulkner, Eudora Welty. The list is long.

I tell my students, Don't dismay. They have the southern gene. The rest of us must labor.

But, in truth, even though it comes naturally to Wendy, she, too, labors. In June she joined me to teach the second session of the yearlong intensive at Mabel Dodge. While the students were on their long afternoon break from one o'clock to four, doing individual practice, writing, sitting, walking, or even napping (deep rest is important), all in silence, Wendy was wrestling with a column. Each afternoon she sat on the patio off the dining room in the same chair, same table, shaded by the enormous cottonwood, leaning over her notebook. Her struggle was palpable. We all could feel it as we passed her on our way to other things. The girl was nailed to the spot. Many of us can't think of words—and she has too many. In each column, she is limited to seven hundred and fifty.

She jokes, "I have to take my writing to Vic Tanny's," an old mid-century gym that made you sweat and was advertised on TV. She has to cinch the belt on her lush writing and get to the point. And she has to figure out what the point is—we all have to do that in our writing, whether thin or fat. She'd like to wax on about Upaya Zen Center, too, but it takes discipline to leave out what is not necessary.

When she mentions a specific plant—Aztec White pole beans or Scarlet Runners—she has a strong urge to spend ten hours studying its history, partly to make sure she gets it right but also out of curiosity—and procrastination. Come to think of it, this is very southern, too. Southerners are wild about history—which can also bog you down in your writing.

We all think of ways to divert ourselves in writing—lately, mine is continually checking that my water and chocolate supply is plentiful. Right in the middle of writing a sentence, I jump up to peruse my stock. These diversions are also a nervousness, an excitement: How long can we bear to be nakedly true? Whatever we are writing, even if it's for a short newsletter article on cement, it's exhilarating to write. And scary. It's saying we care. We have thoughts. We exist.

At the end of the week the students had a lot of compassion for Wendy. They witnessed her labor and were ecstatic when on the last morning she read us her results. She became "our Wendy" and they looked forward to reading the published version, to make sure nothing was edited out.

I encourage you to write. I tell everyone that it is good, important, whole. Yet, to take yourself seriously and have intention in the onslaught of daily life and society is not easy. The only true prescription I can give anyone: Do it. In the face of all inner—and outer—resistance and opposition, just write. Pick up the pen and face yourself.

When I tell Wendy that she is a beautiful writer, her face goes blank. She doesn't believe me. Over the years, once in a while, she has smiled. But I do know she takes pleasure and pride in her work. Like everyone else, she has a gap between who she is and who she thinks she is.

Think about it: do you know someone who is just outright gorgeous? Rarely do they know it. Usually they are even more self-conscious than the rest of us. Or the other extreme—they seem conceited, vain, which underneath is overblown insecurity. Rarely do we meet the mark: we are who we are. No good; no bad. Right on the point. So please, continue. That's what matters.

One other thing about Wendy—and I think this is important: she doesn't read a book, she dives into it. When we teach together she often arrives three days before the workshop or retreat unprepared. In those seventy-two hours she reads the assigned texts. I've watched her think she was in Paris after staying up all night reading *Giovanni's Room* by James Baldwin—or not be able to shake the image of the tiger in Pat Conroy's *Prince of Tides*—she kept looking over her shoulder, where was her new pet now?—or in Kenzaburō Ōe's *A Personal Matter,* she didn't think, *this is different than what I know of the Japanese.* Instead she immersed herself in this one crazy young man's journey. Sure, there is a time for analysis, but loving to read, even when you don't have enough time, is a sign of a writer. Really not just loving to read, but losing yourself, breathing the author's breath is part of it.

Wendy has wild, convoluted family stories. I love to hear them— more, more, I plead. Do you need to visit an old aunt? I'll drive you, I eagerly volunteer. What I want to do is this: lock her up in a room for a year with lots of pens and paper and tell her she can't come out till she has written a long gothic southern novel. I'd feed her two meals a day. Keep her a little hungry. It's good for a writer.

But, Nat, what about all your talk about practice and kind consideration?

The hell with it. I'd sacrifice anything for a good story.

Ikkyu

One Heart, Two Gates

In 1993 a small manila envelope arrived in my box at the Taos post office. A thin volume of eighty pages: *Crow With No Mouth, Ikkyu, Fifteenth-Century Zen Master,* all in bold black letters, versions by Stephen Berg (Copper Canyon Press).

The American Zen teacher George Bowman had sent it. "You don't know Ikkyu?" he said with surprise the last time I'd seen him.

I shook my head. By this time I'd been studying Japanese Zen for nineteen years but was ignorant of Ikkyu. In the note enclosed: *One of the great Rinzai headlights. It's a translation but Ikkyu leaps through anyway.*

Rinzai was a Zen school that studied koans intensely. My original teacher was Soto, "the not-so-bright elderly uncle," Katagiri would half joke. Soto did not emphasize koans.

Standing in the parking lot I read a single poem before I sat high in my '78 Toyota Land Cruiser, pulled out the choke, the body rattling, tires spitting out gravel, and headed for the deep rutted dirt roads leading to the house I'd built of beer cans and tires ten years before. I had lived completely off the grid—no utility companies, no gas lines. A Meyer lemon tree grew in my bedroom and, once a year in November, maybe October, it filled the room with the scent of its white flowers. By Christmas I gave the fruits as gifts, the skin so thin, you bit through and swallowed it.

I was ready to meet Ikkyu and had another ten years on the mesa to contemplate him.

> rain drips from the roof lip
> loneliness sounds like that

I waited two more days before I read another one.

> I can't smell a thing can't see their pink
> but they'll find branches next spring

I was sitting in an overstuffed pink chair when I read that one. I read it again. This was inside out. Not the branch but the blossom, but not the blossom, either. No blossom but it will arrive. Trust in essential emptiness. Nothing there.

I read another:

> born born everything is always born
> thinking about it try not to

I burst out laughing. How we drive ourselves crazy cogitating. I moved deeper into him. Read the whole book. Marked poems I especially liked. All short by this translation—two or three lines. I began to live with Ikkyu. Those weeks and months were ripe green. I felt such gratitude to George for sending them to me.

> only one koan matters
> you

This stung like a bee or stepping on a sharp tack. Koans, hundreds of terse Zen stories each penetrating a different side, angle, dimension of reality. Bam—all distilled to "you." This kaleidoscope we call ourselves. What an enigma. Who can figure it out? Who even wants to? And yet . . . and yet. He turns the finger, nudges our chest, giving us a direct encouragement. In Ikkyu I found an ally, a Zen friend, a comrade. I was not alone.

Any time after those green weeks through the fall—definitely not green in the dry crackling New Mexico landscape, but green inside me—when a friend would call, having a hard time, I'd say, "Hold on I have just the right remedy." I'd run to get Ikkyu. And read to them:

> sick of it whatever it's called sick of the names
> I dedicate every pore to what's here

Sick of the story line, sick of our frontal lobes rambling on, our tired introspection. Instead throwing ourselves into the clear, bright now. I'd get dizzy, high all over again reading him aloud. Friends said it helped. I wonder now if it did.

> I'd love to give you something
> but what would help?

Did my enthusiasm blind me? Forgive me, friends.

> if there's nowhere to rest at the end
> how can I get lost on the way?

To write ultimately you have to go to the life of practice:

> poems should come from bare ground
> night falling on night falling on a black landscape

This is where writing comes from, whether you are at the Iowa Writers' Workshop or making goat cheese on a farm in Wisconsin or on a river raft down the Colorado or on guard, rifle in hand, in Afghanistan.

> books koans sitting miss the heart but not fishermen's songs
> rain pelts the river I sing beyond all of it

Ikkyu's mother was the mistress of the seventeen-year-old emperor and when she became pregnant she had to go into hiding. Her son could not be heir to the throne. At age five Ikkyu was hidden in a Zen monastery for fear of assassination.

By seventeen Ikkyu had a serious, strict Zen master, Keno, with whom he lived and practiced for four years. Just the two of them. When he died, Ikkyu in his grief attempted suicide, but as he was about to drown himself in Lake Biwa, a messenger from his mother interceded and asked, Please go on living for her sake.

Seeking a second master, he found Kaso, another serious teacher. At the age of twenty-seven, while meditating in a rowboat on Lake Biwa, hearing a crow call overhead, he achieved his great awakening. The entire universe became the cawing and he dropped away.

He wrote this poem in response to that experience:

> ten dumb years I wanted things to be different furious proud I
> still feel it
> one summer midnight in my little boat on Lake Biwa
> caaaawwwweeeee
> father when I was a boy you left us now I forgive you

You mean that, when you wake up, see into the center, your father is there? I thought to myself. Do we never get away from our parents?

The crow call brought him back to the heart of the world. Freedom is not rejection, a getting away, but rather a resolution, the sand of our cells settles right down where we are, with the house on the corner, the postman delivering never at the right time, a congresswoman in Arizona shot by a crazy man, King's birthday yesterday, my friend Mary's mother dead today nineteen years, last bit of chocolate on the side table, hair a little dirty and nowhere new to go and nothing special to do in the face of death.

suddenly nothing but grief
so I put on my father's old ripped raincoat

At that time my father was still alive. I loved him mightily and had just finished a big struggle with him. I was torn between great affection and my own will to power—and my rage. The crow called out in the Ikkyu poem, but it didn't affect my father in Florida. Instead the heavy-bodied black raven flapped across the mesa and it changed me.

When Ikkyu left Kaso, he was footloose from age twenty-nine to fifty-seven. That's an unusually long pilgrimage. Time of wandering after awakening is a traditional act, meant to deepen understanding, but as in all things, Ikkyu went beyond any limit. During this period he developed street Zen, out of the monastery and into the living reality of laypeople, who eat meat and fish, drink wine, make love in the middle of poverty and grief. He loved to hang out in brothels and under the bridges with thieves, bums, pirates, wandering women, con artists and there he envisioned his Red Thread Zen, an idea he borrowed from the old Chinese master Kido, linking human beings to birth and death by the red thread of passion and its bloody umbilical cord. To really wake up you have to step out of the cloistered sacred and be in the midst of human life.

Out of this fresh view of Zen, Ikkyu created new forms of calligraphy, poetry, the Noh theater, tea ceremony, and ceramics. The bottom line was sparseness, and stark simplicity in a time of destruction, intrigue, and warring factions.

Ikkyu spoke to the heart and the senses in an era when a desire for power fueled the practice. Ikkyu brought into Japanese Zen a feminine element. No separate sacred realms. Practice was for everyone and included cooking, child care, creating art.

and what is the heart
pine breeze voice in a forgotten painting

At seventy-seven Ikkyu fell in love with Mori, a blind musician in her thirties. He praised her brilliance and celebrated her gifts. This was his great love and he, of course, wrote poems about it.

> and the nights inside you rocking
> smelling the odor of your thighs is everything

> for us no difference between reading eating singing
> making love not one thing or the other

> white-haired priest in his eighties
> Ikkyu still sings aloud each night aloud to himself to the sky
> the clouds
> because she gave herself freely
> her hands her mouth her breasts her long moist thighs

When he was in his eighties, though still unconventional, the Zen authorities asked him to be the abbot of Daitokuji, which was the Kyoto temple in his teacher Kaso's lineage. When Kaso was asked years before who would finally be his successor, almost in dismay at Ikkyu's anarchy but also recognizing his genius, he replied, "It will be the mad one." Now his prophecy was being fulfilled. After so much unrest, all of Kyoto in ruins, Ikkyu was left with the task of rebuilding the temple. His followers in the wealthy merchant class, who were not attacked in the same way as the military and imperial line, stepped forward to help. One of his supporters even cut off the masts from his ship to use as posts for the new construction.

Traditionally, a Zen master writes a poem on his deathbed. This one of Ikkyu's is recited at some Zen gatherings:

> I won't die. I won't go anywhere. I'll be right here.
> Just don't ask anything. I won't answer.

It's Ikkyu's official one, accepted by the Rinzai school. But at the same time he wrote a private death poem that he gave to Mori, his last love.

> I do regret to cease pillowing my head in your lap
> I vow eternity to you

This one is even more like him. Full of juicy feeling.

In 2000 I lived again for eighteen months in Minnesota after years of being away, and one evening in St. Paul a Zen teacher friend and I shared a talk about Ikkyu with about a hundred people who'd never heard of him before. To our surprise, we chose no overlapping poems. I was interested in the more finely attuned awakening poems and the ones that cut through ways of seeing normal reality. He was absorbed by the outrageous sexual ones and the outcries against institutional Zen.

So here's Ikkyu decrying false practice:

> Yaso hangs up ladles baskets useless donations in the temple
> my style's a straw raincoat strolls by rivers and lakes

> They used sticks and yells and other tricks those fakes
> Ikkyu reaches high low like sunlight

We had twenty-one copies of *Crow with No Mouth* to sell and people dashed for them. (I hope you too will dash for a copy.)

When I got back to my friend's house, I sat in the corner of the green couch for a long time with my heavy jacket still on. It was one of those bitter nights in early December, the beginning descent of deep cold, but it was warm in the house. It's just that I couldn't budge to take off the coat. Ikkyu had lived centuries ago and yet I felt him right here. He held no part of himself back.

The Chinese have a saying. Joan Sutherland told it to me. One heart, two gates. When you touch the depths, your life opens in two directions: personal liberation and a need to help the world. That's what I felt in the living room that night—Ikkyu's heart had two gates. Both came from the same source.

Ikkyu is part of my writing life—my sitting, walking, standing life. We carry the people we let sink in deep. This takes time. I will go to my grave loving this squat, rectangular-faced (pug-nosed, doleful-eyed) man, who had the brilliance to radiate out beyond the limits of time, space, and the cold night.

Dogen

Write with the Whole Body

Almost fifteen years ago on a Thursday in the middle of a silent retreat, where we had been sitting for a good part of the morning, I pulled out a TV screen and inserted a blocky VCR cassette—no sleek DVDs at that time—of *Mountains and Rivers: Mystical Realism of Zen Master Dogen.* Dogen, who lived in Japan in the thirteenth century, is a main figure in the Soto Zen lineage of my original teacher. I often quote Dogen and the one quote I'm pretty sure all my students know is "When you walk in the mist, you get wet." Don't struggle to understand practice; show up, be here, and, like osmosis, the teachings will enter your whole body. That's how we learn writing, not through intellectualization, but we write through the whole body. Practice is transmitted physically. Our hands, legs, teeth, butt, eye, brain, nose, heart, knees are taking it in. Then it's really yours. And it has to be yours. No one else can do it for you. And yet, "Do not suppose that what you realize becomes your knowledge and is grasped by your consciousness" (Dogen). You have it; you don't have it. You are free.

The video includes beautiful scenery of mountains and rivers with an original music score in the background overlaid by my dear friend, the late Abbot John Daido Loori, reading Master Dogen's text.

I'd heard the text many times, but it was the first time I'd seen the video and sat absorbed in the visuals, melded with the music and language. At least twenty minutes went by before I thought to glance at the students. When I turned to them, they couldn't contain the still silence another moment. They burst into laughter, tears down their cheeks, falling off their cushions and actually rolling around the floor.

I reached up to pause the video. "What's going on?" I asked in my innocence. "Didn't you all love this?"

Sharyn, a longtime student and a fine singer, began to yodel Dogen's words in an imitation of the video's operatic voice.

Franny, who was the federal public defender for the state of Nevada, said simply, "Where on earth did you get this?"

To this day so many years later all I have to do is mention the video to anyone who had been there and they raise their hands—"Please, I can't take it"—and the old deep laughter rises in them.

I should mention that the video won an award, to let you know I wasn't completely off. What I don't think the students understood is that intense practice like we were doing that week, juxtaposed with Dogen's words, can send minds illogically, madly, wildly flying. In the middle of a silent retreat where regular social mores are broken, where you step out of the norm of daily life, the question often comes up: "Am I nuts? What am I doing here?" But it also gives us the opportunity to see the world in a bigger way, unconstrained by habit and comfort and a certain social organization that is efficient but often can be numbing and blinding.

And here was Dogen suddenly planted in the center of their open minds. Shall I give you a bit of Mountains and Rivers Sutra so that you may taste what they were listening to?

> You should reflect on the moment when you see the water of the ten directions as the water of the ten directions. This is not just studying the moment when human and heavenly beings see water; this is studying the moment when water sees water. This is a complete understanding. You should go forward and backward and leap beyond the vital path where other fathoms other.

Laughter can come from a deep place. A recognition of something meeting something. Open mind meeting open mind. The mind of practice meeting the mind of Dogen's thirteenth-century practice. Time no longer exists. The laughter was a final answer to the question, Am I nuts? Certainly you are. And how happy we are to be together in it, that someone is mirroring our true minds. And that is exactly what Dogen is doing.

He is not explaining realization here, as if it were a separate object to be discussed and examined. Dogen is calling out from the center and using language in a new way to communicate what being awake is like. It is the direct transmission through language.

Sometimes a crow call above your head, a pebble hitting bamboo breaks open the world. But here Dogen is using words (attention, writers!) to transmit the world beyond words. Can there be a world beyond words? Well, he's certainly giving us a world in words.

But this writing is not for us to decipher. You are not going to decipher it. But you can become it. That's really how we learn anyway— the kind of learning that sticks. It moves through your whole body; we absorb it through all our cells, not just the brain.

> You should study the green mountains, using numerous worlds as your standard. You should clearly examine the green mountains' walking and your own walking. You should also examine walking backward and backward walking and investigate the fact that walking forward and backward has never stopped since the very moment before form arose, since the time of the King of the Empty Eon.

In 1990 for the full year I met once a week with a group of writers in Santa Fe. We were all friends and for fun we delegated Eddie, one of us, as the teacher and wrote together on any topic, trying to bend toward fiction.

One week only five of the ten showed up. John wanted to read from James Salter's novel *Light Years,* which he had almost memorized word for word. Then someone else pulled out a book she loved and read from it.

"Wait a minute," I said and went into the bedroom, where I had Arnie Kotler and Kaz Tanahashi's translation of Dogen's *Mountains and Rivers Sutra.* "Listen to this." The crew had followed me into the bedroom. All sat on the bed, but me. I stood to recite Dogen, moving my body in the ecstasy of his words. Did I know what they meant? I recognized their wonder. I've been known to let language blow over me. You don't keep stopping and asking what the wind is saying, do you? You let it blow.

When I was done, John, Eddie, Rob, and another friend were all looking up at me in consternation, their faces crunched, heads tilted at an angle: Huh?

You don't get it? I asked.

No, they shook their heads.

Okay, I read more. Just listen.

It is not only that there is water in the world, but there is a world in water. It is not just in water. There is also a world of sentient beings in clouds. There is a world of sentient beings in the air. There is a world of sentient beings in fire. There is a world of sentient beings on earth. There is a world of sentient beings in the phenomenal world.

I was rocking out.

My friends, alas, were not. These people were smart, real smart. And Dogen left them flat. I understood then in a way I never had before that my writing life had turned a corner a long time ago, that it had gone down a path not necessarily the path the best minds would go down. From then on I understood the proclivity toward scrambling my mind and that it may be different from the desire to write, though for me they were one and the same.

The first weekend in May 2011, Joan Halifax organized a Dogen weekend at Upaya Zen Center to celebrate Kaz Tanahashi's ten-year work of translating and publishing the *Treasury of the True Dharma Eye: Zen Master Dogen's Shobogenzo*.

Henry Shukman, a writing friend and a fellow teacher, was the first to speak on the panel.

He began by recalling the time in 1990 he saw me stomp around my patio reciting Dogen. (I thought for sure it was my bedroom.) "I'd never heard of Dogen before. And when I heard him I was speechless. My mouth went dry. I disappeared."

"So you were the fourth person that night who all these years I could not remember? No wonder. You weren't there." Everything made sense. Though Henry, too, continued to write and publish, he also over the years pursued Zen, retreat after retreat, sitting till his head grew bald.

Peter Levitt, poet and Zen teacher, was next on the panel to speak. He talked about how Dogen was "the love guru." Hearing love and Dogen together was a delight, reminding us Dogen was revealing understanding from all his pores.

"We should start a band and call it 'The Dogenettes,'" I intoned.

The truth is, over the years Dogen could also become maddening. We weren't always broken open when we read him. We fell on the side of trying to understand too hard and when we failed to decipher, "Mountains do not lack the qualities of mountains. Therefore, they always abide in ease and always walk," we wanted to bang our heads against a stone wall.

My teacher, Katagiri Roshi, one of the three Japanese Zen masters to whom the new *Shobogenzo* translation is dedicated, often discussed Dogen in his Wednesday evening and Saturday morning lectures, which could go on for two hours. His dutiful students made gallant effort to keep our legs crossed, backs straight for the full time, while our minds screamed and a great aggression developed toward this thirteenth-century Zen master who seemed to create our suffering.

Peter cited Dogen's large, allowing, magnanimous mind. How reading him gave Peter permission to be himself. And I thought how reading Dogen also gave us permission to drop ourselves. I have loved the Genjo koan by Dogen from the moment I read it. "To study the awakened way is to study the self. To study the self is to forget the self. To forget the self is to be actualized by myriad things."

The month before I'd taught in Madison, Wisconsin, and my student Miriam Hall told me something Henry Rollins, lead singer of Rollins Band, had said. This is a close paraphrase: Hating someone's guts is like shitting in your own hand and then eating it.

That is a direct teaching, I thought. Graphic, to the point—and true.

I quoted it to the group when it was my turn on the panel. Dead silence ensued. I repeated it again and explained how when I heard that quote it reminded me of the circular thinking, the direct transmission of Dogen's truth. The group was still aghast. "Oh, stop being such prudes. Zen is not the Lutherans sitting zazen. It's outside—or inside—all that. Didn't you know Dogen wrote pages on how much toilet paper you should use to wipe yourselves: a single square."

We can carry on about how great someone is but we should not be frozen. Whatever our idea, it does not exactly hit the mark. The mark is zero. No separation. We are the mountains and the rivers.

At the Dogen weekend I read some of Dogen aloud, the way I did to my writing friends, to let them feel the rhythm of his speech. I had participants write three or four ordinary short sentences at the top of the page and then had them scramble up the words for about seven minutes as a mirroring of Dogen's use of language. "People speak this way because they think that it must be impossible to exist without having a place on which to rest" (Dogen). If we split open the structure of grammar, something new can be revealed, energy can be released, and we can discover a fresh foundation, a new way "to rest."

Peter thought I'd asked for four words to use over and over again in different ways. So for this exercise, try words or short sentences, either or both.

These are the words Peter chose: *children, garden, silence, music.* And this is what he wrote:

> Silence grows a garden of musical children,
> each one shouting no word.
> Deep in the heart of a silent child
> the music never stops flowing.
> To say that the child hears her garden
> is to understand a silent child.
> To say that you understand a silent child
> is to miss her music.
> A child seeds a child, and only a child can
> be one. If you think a garden is not also
> a child, ask the silence one more time.
> If you think the time of asking is not the music,
> a silent child will begin singing.
> The music is the teaching of silence—
> the growing of a child,
> the garden of weeping
> the stillness of wind in a shadow.
> When you realize a child, you realize a garden.
> When you realize a garden, you realize a child.
> This is the music unplayed.
> This is the music playing.

In Kaz's beautiful introduction, he explains that Dogen, who is Japanese, makes his own translations of Chinese texts, sometimes stretching and developing his own thoughts and expanding the meaning. For instance, a line of poetry by Rujing is normally translated, "Plum blossoms open in early spring," but Dogen translates it, "Plum blossoms open early spring." Do you see the difference, the dynamism, the alive muscle, the unique perspective of the second translation?

And you know how we use the ordinary phrase "for the time being"? (For the time being, she will continue to eat oatmeal.) From Dogen's interpretation of a verse by Yaoshan (ninth-century Chinese), "For the time being, stand on a high mountain . . . ," Tanahashi tells us, Dogen developed his understanding that time is no other than being. You can see the deep attention Dogen was paying to language.

At the end of the weekend I shyly approached Kaz Tanahashi to ask him to sign the two-volume translation of Dogen. I've been acquainted with Kaz over the years but in that moment I felt a mixture of pride, gratitude—an immense acknowledgment of the task he had accomplished—and I felt humbled. In order to give us such a fine translation, he had to turn himself inside out, to become completely drenched, saturated in Dogen so there was no longer a gap, a space between the two men. That's what love knows. You are the treasure you are dedicated to.

He signed with a special black pen, "Thank you for your contribution to the book"—I'd helped a bit with translation—and then, "Enjoy your enlightenment!" Pure Dogen. Once awakened, you are free from the distinction of those who are awake and those who aren't. You see awakening in everyone. Kazuaki Tanahashi now passes it on to us.

Gwen

Closing the Gap

A student who has studied with me for sixteen years has can-cer. After all her chemotherapy treatments she found out the night we had dinner together that she was in remission.

"I'm going to live. I'm going to live," she said over and over at the dinner table, jerking her shoulders up to her ears. At fifty-four a person in this country is still young.

She was so exuberant, I became high, too—not just from my happiness for her, but from being in contact with someone so fully aware of both her death and her gift of more time. It was a poignantly full experience.

The tumors grew back with a vengeance after four weeks. All that vigor that Gwen had—cancer now was using it to grow.

She wrote an email to her group of writing friends.

> Women,
> First, let me express my gratitude for your support and friend-ship in my life. I was so encouraged during these last 6 months by your emails, cards, and letters.
>
> Then, I must tell you that the doc found new tumors of the cancer on her physical exam yesterday. They were not there 6 weeks ago on the ct and they are large already. She told me it was time to quit work, offered me some palliative chemotherapy to

control the symptoms, and basically let me know I have a very limited time left to walk this wonderful earth.

So if you could turn your requests towards a peaceful, comfortable death for me, I would appreciate it.

I have loved you all.

Gwendolyn

One of them (these were all students of mine) forwarded it to me. That's how Gwen was. I had been her teacher and she was shy with me, uncertain. The first pronouncement, even of her first discovery of cancer, came through someone else. Then when I reached out, we wrote back and forth, especially what we thought death was. An afterlife? Cold into the grave? Some secret watching of those still alive? She hoped she'd still be connected.

I went to visit her in Las Vegas, New Mexico, where she lived far out on a ranch—I had to cross a wide stream and drive a narrow dirt road with a steep drop on my left. I brought her a violet scarf for her bald head. I was used to bald heads. All the priests at the Zen center, as far back as my beginning thirties, shaved their heads. She looked beautiful. But this was all before our dinner and the remission.

Now it was different. No remission. I wrote her two lines, telling her I love her, have always loved her, that she is with me every moment and how can I help?

Then I went crazy. Would she write me back this time, too, in her step-backward approach to communicating with me? She has said each time it is hard to tell me and prefers group communication with the others. All day—it was a Thursday—I wanted to *do* something. Kill her cancer. Rip her from this scenario. We could go on a trip, run away. I hacked at a tree in my backyard that had grown scraggly last summer. It was mid-March. Spring had come early with little snow all winter.

At a nursery on that Thursday I selected and paid for nine rosebushes that the nursery would hold and coddle for another six weeks until they are ready for planting in May. A simple green ceramic birdbath sat in front of the parking lot. I bought that, too, though I didn't need it. I began making chicken soup at eight at night and didn't finish the cooking till almost midnight. Then I decided to make green rice with fresh herbs. I went digging in the garden for chives in the dark.

What was I doing? Living harder for the both of us. But nothing helped. Because what I wanted was to help her, not myself. What else can one do when someone is dying? It's the hardest of all to sit there and let life and death happen no matter how you rail or what you cook.

What does someone dying have to say good-bye to? I look around. Every single detail seems important. The old yellow tennis ball on the cement floor at the base of the wall, the wall, the light switch, the door, the wood chest. The chair, the table, all those books, all those words. No more.

Gwen was the emergency doctor at the Las Vegas hospital. She was fast and smart. They needed her there.

"I don't want to leave Robin," she told me when there was still hope. Robin was the first and only woman she'd ever been with, now for ten years. They had developed a three-thousand-acre ranch together with the hope of conducting workshops on the land to empower women.

Early Friday her email popped up on the screen.

Natalie,

    If you can, I would like to see you again before I go. I'm still getting chemo in hopes it will make the time easier, the doc told me it won't make it longer, otherwise Robin and I are here every day.

    Thank you for not leaving me in this.

    Gwen

I wrote her right back: What day?
Another email popped up:

> Maybe the next week. Post chemo Thursday is a bad day physically for me

I talk a lot about death in class, but I don't know anything about it. No idea about how one should die, what age, what circumstance. What happens. Maybe that's an advantage. I have no opinion.

Except one: I know to shut up when I need to. Really, I want to whisper, howl, scream, whine, plead, please don't die. As if a person had a choice. No one does. Everyone dies—sometime, eventually. No one gets out of it.

Look around: flowers die, trees lose their leaves, dogs get run over, cats kill mice. Our grandfathers, our great-grandmothers, Lincoln, Washington, Harriet Tubman: they are all dead now. Even cars die. The people who came over on the *Mayflower* and the survivors of World War I are dead. Yet, we don't get it. We think we are separate. It can't happen to us.

In my early years of practice, a Zen story absolutely riveted me:

> Many centuries ago it was a time of terrible unrest in the East. Thieves, mercenaries, bandits roamed freely. A Zen monastery was nestled deep in the mountains and many novices studied there under a great Zen master.
>
> Word traveled that a band of runaway soldiers were heading toward the monastery. All the monks panicked, feared for their lives and quickly took off into the surrounding hills. When the pirate army arrived, they kicked open doors and the place was empty. They were furious, hungry to kill and conquer.
>
> The general broke open a passageway a little removed from the rest and found the Zen master sitting quietly, studying the scriptures in front of him.

The general stepped forward and stood over him. The teacher looked up, "Yes, can I help you?"

The captain unsheathed his sword and held it high. "With this, do you realize I can run you through."

The Zen master replied calmly, "Yes, I can be run through."

The captain bowed, put his sword away and left the room.

The master was undeterred. I marveled, *that's the way to save myself,* to be victorious over death. (I was very young.)

A few years later I heard a similar story, but this time a different Zen master—Yantou—was run all the way through with the sword. He did scream loud enough, it is rumored, that he was heard for thirty miles away—he met his death—but still he died. Knowing in his heart and bones about death didn't save him. Maybe he didn't think about being saved. Maybe really knowing about death you understand there's no saving, no saving account.

I planned that this time when I went to Las Vegas to see Gwen, I would hold the meeting outside the realm of hope. It was the only fair way.

Another email is forwarded:

Ladies,

As I approach the veil, I am becoming anxious that I haven't made a difference in this world. Debbie wrote me an email, remembering things about our friendship, and telling me how knowing me helped and changed her. I printed it out, and will ask Robin to read it to me on my death bed. I thought I would ask y'all to write me something like that, so I can go to the other side encouraged that I did do something good in this life.

Thank you.

Gwendolyn

When my Zen teacher was dying, he received many letters from around the country, telling him what he had meant and how he had helped.

His wife read them aloud to him.

He turned his head to her on the white sheets and said, "I didn't think I did very much. Maybe I did help a little."

Human beings have a gap—between who we think we are and who we really are. Closing the gap is what being awake is. Those letters helped Katagiri. Sure, he had a lot of what was awake in him, but at vulnerable moments we need each other's support. Gwen was now asking for that help on her deathbed.

When Thich Nhat Hanh, the Vietnamese Buddhist teacher, was visiting a good friend who was dying, he stood at the foot of his bed and held the man's feet: Remember when we did that peace walk down Fifth Avenue? He recalled to his friend detailed good memories they had shared that affirmed his friend's life.

At an evening seminar, soon after I read Gwen's request for affirmation, Joan Sutherland read these death poems from Grace Schireson's *Zen Women*.

> In the autumn of my sixty-sixth year, I've already lived a long time—
> The intense moonlight is bright upon my face.
> There's no need to discuss the principles of koan study;
> Just listen carefully to the wind outside the pines and cedars.
>
> —*Ryonen*

> My final message:
> Flowers blooming
> with all their heart
> in lovely Sakurai Village.
>
> —*Rengetsu*

In Zen at your death it is a tradition to write a poem, an illumination upon approaching personally the Great Mystery. Books have been published with death poems of great Zen masters. I have often paged through them looking for my own clarification, but I realize now they'd all been written by men. I unconsciously never considered writing one.

But now I immediately thought, *What will I write?* Then, *Forget it. My time will come soon enough.*

What will Gwen write?

I send the poems to her. And she writes back thanking me.

I plan to drive out the following Tuesday after her first "palliative chemo to control symptoms." We don't know how long she has. She hopes she survives to May 1, Robin's fiftieth birthday.

I drive out even-minded through the long, open country, thinking this might be the last time I see her. I'm ready for any state of decline she's in.

I walk down the hall past the kitchen into the living room. She's beaming, sitting cross-legged on the couch. "Natalie, I wrote all morning."

I sidle next to her, not expecting this.

She tells me how she and Nancy are working on their books every morning and emailing their progress to each other. She tells me about the book she has begun that recounts how she and Robin settled the land and about the history of the land back to the 1800s, when a woman with her thirteen children lived alone on the ranch.

"Their cemetery is out back. It's where I'm going to be buried, too."

"Gwen, you are full of energy."

"It's from writing—and that chemo which slowed the tumors. You know, you said we'll go out writing, that's our commitment. Remember you said that?"

(Yes, I'd said that as an example of determination but never quite expected to see the raw actuality in front of me.)

I needed a moment to catch this new rhythm. "So you've been

writing a lot?" A pause. "Well, of course, when you're concentrating in writing you are not alive or dead—you're deathless."

"That's it. That's it." She nods her head up and down. I notice the typed pages on her coffee table.

I gesture with my chin toward them. "So read to me."

In all the years of working together I've heard little of her work. She was shy to read aloud in class and mostly the students read to each other and I get out of the way. They learn to not look to me for approval or disapproval. From the beginning they are on their own—and with each other. And yet I know people love to be listened to. "Go on, from the beginning."

"Really?" She picks up the sheets and reads the introduction, which moves back and forth between Ignacita, the original settler, and her and Robin, settling the land in the twenty-first century.

It was midwinter when we came to live with the land. Cottonwood branches scraped a gunmetal sky in a roaring canyon wind. Ignacita heated her hut with juniper. We heat the ruins of her last son's stone house with the same. It was bone cold for all of us.

She was short and brown, genizaro, a mixed race of Spanish and Native American. I am taller than she and white, my curly hair a sign of my storied ancestry.

Ignacita could not read or write. I am a physician poet.

She had black hair. I had brown. Eventually, we both went gray.

She spoke Spanish. I speak English.

She had to fight to keep this land. I have looked for it all my life.

She was married, had thirteen children. I am childless by choice, and cannot legally marry my partner.

She washed her clothes once a week in the rectangular tank by the dance hall. I take my laundry to town.

I ride a horse for pleasure. She worked them to stay alive.

She ate the corn, beans and squash she grew. I am a convicted carnivore.

I wear pants. She wore dresses.

Her nineteen hundred head of sheep overgrazed the land, began the accelerated erosion I work to heal.

Her husband herded sheep. She stayed home. I drive twenty-seven miles to work the ER, amid the technology she never had, the technology that has failed us.

I will be buried on sweat lodge hill. Ignacita's bones lie under the chapel floor.

She's dead. I'm alive.

No one knows our stories.

"Holy Mackerel," I said. (I can't help it—I am so corny.) "Where did you ever learn to write like that?"

She laughs—even giggles—in delight.

"Read me more."

It was raining sideways. Water streamed in under the eave, ran down the mud plaster covering the sandstone walls, threatened to dissolve the adobe mortar that holds the one-room building together. By the light of oil lamps we bought from Lehman's non-electric catalog, in the deafening din of rain pounding on the tin roof, we looked at each other, wondering how two women physicians could be living the twenty-first century as if it were 1887.

Sometimes you have to go back before you can go forward. Like a slingshot, the further you pull back, the further things fly when you let go. Robin and I went so far back that we're living the future today.

My love of the desert began when I was ten. On summer vacation treks from the humid swamps of Louisiana to the uncles' houses in crowded California, I inhaled the surprise of such a thing as a hot, dry wind. I expanded into the power of a solitary campsite beside Tuttle Creek. I marveled at the novel idea of a log cabin that didn't rot or become entombed by rampant vegetation in the century since a pioneer abandoned it. I saw there was another way to live by watching the saguaro cactus march up rocky mountains and fade out where the Joshua trees began.

I moved to New Mexico when I was forty-two. On my days off from working the Emergency Room, I went hiking in tank tops and shorts in February. Dry, sandy washes held fossilized shells. Trails through cow pastures lead to saddles in wind battered ridges. Broad Canyon offered the solace of deep silence. I began to spend entire days sitting in the crevices of the red walls of the canyon. I heard swallowtail butterflies flap their enormous yellow wings. Hummingbirds left the red flowering ocotillos to hover in front of my face, trying to figure out what I was. Pondering petroglyphs, analyzing bones from the den of a ring tailed cat, I spent months in Broad Canyon remembering who I was.

Sitting on the cool rock in the shade of the canyon, I was seized by the idea that I could buy remote land like Broad Canyon, and offer other women this empowering experience of connecting with their deepest selves in a wilderness setting.

The first summer in New Mexico, I went to a work party where a gigantic ER nurse took off her shirt and stood under the desert sun in her bra five minutes after she arrived. Standing back from the action beside the pool, I met Robin, a tall pediatrician with gentle hands, and long, wavy hair. She walked over to talk with me because she saw I was alone. Robin came to the party with her partner, another ER doc. We commented on the shocking behavior of the people I worked with at a party like this. When men started throwing fully clothed women in the pool, Robin and I wandered away together.

I remember walking by a sandy embankment, talking about horses. I had just begun riding lessons. Robin had been riding since she was eight. We both felt more comfortable around horses than people.

For a full hour she reads and I listen.

Robin comes home. Robin has researched on the Web how to build a simple coffin and driven the hour and a half into Santa Fe to go to Home Depot.

When she brought the materials to the cashier, the young man cheerily said, "Looks like you are going to build something."

"A coffin." Robin said the words before she thought.

The kid blanched, threw his eyes down, and didn't look up again through the whole transaction.

On the wide windowsill Gwen points out the things she has selected to be buried with her. A raggedy stuffed panda bear from her childhood in Louisiana, the violet scarf I gave her, a collection of poems by Mary Oliver, *Leap* by Terry Tempest Williams, her Dr. Teekell name tag that she plans to have pinned to her nightgown along with a pin proclaiming her a Fellow of the American College of Emergency Physicians, her leather aviator hat with coyote trim, the prologue to her book, and her walking stick.

Death becomes matter-of-fact, ordinary, nothing to run from.

"We've talked out everything." Robin wants to continue to live on the land, even though she'll be alone.

"I told her I want her to find love again." She smiles at Robin. "As long as I'm always number one."

I stay for three hours, even drink Coke with Gwen, and she is pleased I join her. She has cases stored by the refrigerator.

"Please come and see me again."

I promise I will and leave energized. What a great visit and then as I drive back across the river and the shadows grow long, it comes home to me: she is dying. After she is buried in the fine coffin, she will be dead. She won't be back. I imagine the long hours alone for Robin on the land. I feel tired. My chest squeezes tight.

As the car muddles along the dirt road and I stop to open and close three gates on the way, I recall the second silent July retreat I ever did at Mabel Dodge. Late in the week, people were very settled. We carpooled to Penitente Lane, drove down the dirt road to park and walk to the Morada, a Penitente church, the religion long banned, an inlet on the vast Pueblo land with a narrow path through sage, juniper, and piñon. At each end of the walk is a large wood cross, each fifteen feet high, that the religious carried on their backs. To the north you can see the entire Taos Mountain, sacred to Taos Pueblo nestled at the foot, and to the southwest in the distance you can see the flat-topped Pedernal, a hundred miles away in Abiquiu, New Mexico. Georgia O'Keeffe made a bargain with God about this mountain. If she painted it enough, it would be hers. Her ashes are on top of it.

After parking we gather at the Morada and, lifting a black plastic tarp covering bricks, I explain adobe. "Each one weighs about forty pounds. A mixture of dirt, water, sand, and straw, poured into rectangular molds, and baked in the sun, which is so strong here, it makes a durable mud brick."

We begin slow walking from one black cross by the Morada to the chipped white cross. Every once in a while in our slow, half-hour walk, I ring a small bell and we pause, arms at sides, for three breaths, reminding us to slow down the forward-propelling motion of our minds, which have suddenly sunk their teeth into a direction, that cross at the other end. We remember to come back to one step, then the placement of another.

When we finally do arrive, I point out in the vast distance the line of dark trees at an angle across Taos Mountain. "It leads to Blue Lake, holy to the Tewa people. Outsiders who are not in the tribe are not allowed on the mountain. For a hundred and fifty years the U.S. Forest Service controlled the lands, where white people hunted and fished, but Nixon signed the land back to the Pueblo. They love Nixon."

Sometimes I point out to the west the rounded, wide San Antonio Mountain, where wild herds of elk roam, and sometimes I point to a scraggly big elm, the only tall tree nearby. "And that's the tree where Banana Rose had an awakening experience," I say, referring to my 1995 novel by the same name.

But I don't think I explained all this on that second retreat at Mabel's because by the time we reached the cross it was pitch black. Given to unplanned spontaneous acts while teaching, as I was about to ring the bell for evening meditation, I said, "Let's walk to the cross," not coordinating the dimming light, nor telling anyone to bring a flashlight. The pueblo has no electricity—they try to keep it the original way—and there was not even a distant glow to rely on. Everyone froze, realizing we had no way back.

Gwen, who I now remember was on that walk, sidled up to me and in Gwen fashion of knowing all kinds of information, details, coordinates, whispered, "A full moon tonight, should rise within an hour."

I lit up and turned to the group. "We will stand here and wait for the full moon to rise." I looked back at Gwen and she gestured to the rising vicinity, east of Taos Mountain over a high hump of hill. "Over there," I pointed, imitating Gwen's direction.

We stood in a line, arms at sides, no one stirring, heads tilted up, waiting a full forty minutes. Have you ever waited in the dark not sure when light would come? It was a long, long time. Our patience was big and after a while we stood in eternity and the moon would come when it came. As the bungled leader, I rested in the faith of Gwen's knowledge and slowly, slowly the mountain grew a faint glow like a soft spray of water. And we watched as it amplified, extending, taking its slow time.

Then all at once—pop—the full white globe exploded over the mountain. Simultaneously, the coyotes began to howl and the drums beat at the pueblo clear across the empty space. We turned, our path was lit and we walked home in moonlight.

Gwen died June 23, 2011, almost exactly ten years later.

One week before she died, Beth Howard drove from Cheyenne,

Wyoming, to visit Gwen for a day. (In the West, we travel long distances to visit friends.) As Beth was leaving, Gwen leaned on her elbow and said, "Let me give you two instructions from this angle: One"—she crooked a finger—"live every single minute. You don't know how long you have."

"Two: if there is something you want to do, do it *now,* don't wait. I thought I'd hold off real writing till I retired. When I heard my terminal diagnosis I realized in that instant all I ever really wanted to do was write."

Blue Chair

Creating Texture

I have just drawn a fat chair smack in the middle of a big piece of paper. The kind of chair you want to nestle in, write a book about love in, with lots of sex in unlikely places, in the back of a bus, down an empty alley behind a Dumpster, in the room next to your dying mother. Or plant yourself in front of a window, sitting in it, for an entire winter of mornings, watching endless snow, drinking black tea and eating a single pink cupcake to spite health and the cold. Maybe you hang your legs over the substantial arms of the chair and learn to whistle or sing Irish folk songs. In other words, it's a good chair that takes up almost the whole page.

Now I take my paints and go for it. I'm using gouache, water based but not transparent like watercolors, where the light goes through the color onto the page. With gouache the paint is opaque. Light does not go through it. I have little cakes and I have tubes. I begin with turquoise. But the turquoise looks thin on paper, so I swing the paintbrush over to red and glob it on heavy all over the chair, which does not become red because it has turquoise underneath. I try green, then a cerulean blue, then I take a leap—to an opera high pink. I squeeze out some magenta, all the while adding more water to the brush. I alternate from the cakes in a row to tubes. What am I doing, other than sidestepping a mess? Building texture till the chair purrs and looks like velvet. What color is it now? I'm not sure if it is a green, a blue, a purple? It is all of those, but not in patches, more the way anything is if you look at it long enough. One color is made up of many colors. Even my black chair, I turn my head, it's by my writing table, right now at 7 A.M. has a glow of pale yellow light on it reflected through the window from the building next door. But the chair in the painting, whatever color, is now present on the page, lush, glowing, beckons. The texturing sprung it alive.

Now what do I do? I add in striped, flowered wallpaper in back of it and a plant of mother-in-law tongues in a pot to the right. I add a birdcage up above with three blue birds, one on a swing, but I want more birds. I draw in two more, but on the floor to the back of the chair, each escapee heads off in an opposite direction. The floor becomes wooden by adding lines. Now I'm going to pile up some books helter-skelter near the legs of the chair. This is a literary painting: *Hemingway, McCullers, Zweig, Baldwin,* I scrawl on the spines in black ink.

I remember this November 2011 is the twenty-fifth anniversary of *Writing Down the Bones,* my first book. Under the right front leg of the chair, I draw an open spiral notebook with indecipherable scrawl, but you can see the title of the chapter "Man Eats a Car" (which is in the book) and every other line or so a word emerges: *go, hunger, you, write, Katagiri.* The painting has become secret homage to a book that was written in this chair. I add on the left on the floor a cup of hot chocolate and that pink cupcake in silver paper with a red cherry on top.

Most of these objects—notebook, books, cup, birdcage, muffin— get only one chance at color, a yellow, a green, the bluebirds get a dark blue from an old color cake in my box. Even the red flowers on the wallpaper—a single dab of red in the center, and a dark orange for the petals. These details I add are in primary colors, one or two washes, not the deep texture like the chair, the centerpiece, the thing that has gravity, presence, deep dimension, that holds the story. The details around it are human delight, charming fluff, transitory nature, like in a memoir the details point to the structure, which is the chair, the driving force, the reason the whole thing is happening.

Why am I telling you this? Over time you learn to cultivate texture, a richness to what you write, adding layers, where you can almost feel the plush velvet; your words translate into a sensate material, with the wind out the window, the red of day and the sweet, sour smell of tar on the roof.

A student recently came forward. "I finished a ten-minute writing practice and said to myself, *You know, it's good, you should really develop this.* As soon as I said that I went dead. All the enthusiasm drained out."

I asked, "What if you drop the word *develop* and said instead to add texture and detail, color it in?"

She bobbed her head up and down. Yes, yes.

The word *develop* has been overused for mandatory school compositions. Our minds clutch.

Last week Ren wrote about exiting a small town in Utah and seeing a flying saucer. Immediately if she said that term *flying saucer* we would have written it off. Yeah, yeah, and my mother had wings. (Writers can be terribly cynical.) But she didn't say that. Instead she ever so slowly described the unfolding landscape, the low hills, the heavy clouds, patches of brush, the glint in the distance. And she began with the phrase "I know it happened." What happened? We were waiting. Her partner was in the car with her and her partner had a can of Diet Coke. That Coke can was the primary color against the shades and textures, the slow buildup of something you're not sure of, far off, she's not sure of either, but she is. And she never mentions that *saucer* word, never names it. She doesn't need to. We all feel it lift off, unknown and unaccountable. We hold on to that dab of Coke, that dot of something familiar as we are lifted into the surprising air of mystery and belief.

As Ren read this piece aloud, we could also feel Nebraska, where she was raised, in the understatement, the acute attention, almost a rancher or farmer's, to the quality of air and what it portends. We could feel the loneliness of her childhood, the disappointment and disbelief, lift up as something in the distant hills slowly makes its presence known. Girl from Nebraska City, home of Arbor Day and a cold mother, leans across the dashboard of her car outside of Denver into another world. All of it is there.

Then sometimes the texturing comes when you think you have finished a story and later another patch of it appears. My student Gwen has died and I think it's the end. Then her partner, Robin, visits on a late Wednesday morning after she's done errands in town for the ranch. For two months now Robin has been alone on those three thousand acres and in my whole life I've never seen grief so stamped on a handsome face. But we don't talk of that. They have two chicken houses, one for the layer hens and one where the chicks now are pullet size, almost three-quarters grown. Two days ago Robin, dressed to drive into Las Vegas for her pediatrician shift, stops to check on the chicks, opens the door to find thirty-four of them with heads torn off, breasts ripped open, blood and feathers strewn all over and the one survivor that had been outside, screeching, stepping over the dead bodies.

Robin in her office suit grabs the live one under her arm and in shock throws her into the other henhouse, hoping she's big enough to survive, climbs in her truck, already late, knowing she has back-to-back patient appointments, and turns the vehicle in a wide angle—who could have done this?—she sees bear paws on the wall outside and then glares at the metal frame of the small high window, bent out of place. A drought all summer has bears desperate for food before they go into hibernation. All over the state, animal control has been swamped by calls to catch them.

Later at work Robin finds on the Internet that bears eat the livers and heads of chickens. That night she digs a deep hole with the backhoe and buries thirty-four bodies. Her neighbor tells her to get a shotgun. "Once they break in, they won't stop."

"I've been a vegetarian since 1979, now I'm going to become a bear killer?" she tells me over mint tea.

Ten days later I receive an email: over the last week the same rogue bear climbed up the cistern, crossed the roof, slid down the porch, smashed in a window, and killed all but eight of the laying hens, including the one pullet who'd been relocated. The following night he came back to finish what he'd started, leaving only a single traumatized survivor, whom Robin took to a friend's flock in Mora. All the alley cats but one were also killed. He'd been back every night since. "I am now spending my nights in the pickup truck cradling a shotgun and wanting it to be over."

So far their paths have not crossed.

In the next paragraph of her email she lists the subtitle suggestions by the local publisher, who is planning to publish Gwen's book, the one she finished in her last three months, titled *The Winter Years*. Robin tells me at tea how Gwen plotted, outlined, agonized over the book for years, but when she heard she was dying she dropped all thought and burned through.

"Oh, Gwen," I say, looking up at the ceiling, "never have I wanted you to return so badly. I want to point out that you finished the way I taught you. Three months—Go."

Both Robin and I laugh, but it comes home deeper that I don't get to say any more; what was said, was said, though the knowledge of her death ripples long after the final stone dropped, rich and living on.

Cannot Write This Alone

It's Monday night and I have driven across town, down Alameda, left at Paseo, but not a quick left, the gray car in front of me stalled. I had to wait through a green arrow and then the full green light and another long red. After making it to Paseo, I drove, not knowing why I was going to this writing group I am a member of but never go to, because I'm writing a book and don't want to race my hand across the page and suffer my mind's thoughts. I need direction, chapters, ideas. But in the last two weeks I've noticed the studio where I write, where I have four kinds of chocolate bars and two rolls of Droste chocolate circles, a whole row of a bookshelf for my sweets, where I have my old torn fat chair from the mesa in Taos and a table and a white-tiled bathroom, a painting on the wall of Minneapolis I sold in 1980 for fifty dollars at my first art show, bought back in 2010 for five hundred dollars, a watercolor Wendy Johnson painted as a young Zen student practicing at Tassajara of the waterfall there and I have another painting of a Buddha with an airplane and a cat that an old student Andrew Hudson from Washington, D.C., did, piles of notebooks, my worn copy of *Ballad of the Sad Café*, and the large dictionary my parents bought me for twenty-five dollars when they first visited my home in Taos. They said, let us buy you something, and I said I need a dictionary.

"A dictionary?" my father said with the same expression of disbelief he had when I wanted a microscope in fifth grade and a chemistry set in sixth grade.

And I have pens, a whole box of them, and a yoga mat on the floor to stretch on when my lower back gets tight.

But for all that, in the last week and a half I do not want to go in there. I know all about resistance, how even when you want something bad like I want to write this manuscript, how just before you are about to do it, a cement wall flies up or a heaviness in the arms, a weariness in the eyes and you ask yourself, *Is this all I will do with this one great life? Write book after book?* I know all about this, how to turn that push away as a push far into the middle of the page, but this is not resistance. It's a cold chamber, the walls white, I have nothing to say and I am not blocked. I don't believe in that. You pick up the pen and go.

I know really it is not the studio. I could go to the library, a café. The days grow longer into July and I am carrying something behind words and I do not write. Last Wednesday I walked over to the Zen center to hear the lecture. I yawned and wiggled through most of it. Right near the end the presenter quoted from Case 36 of the Iron Flute: Where will I find you after you die? Hearing that line, my body jerked up. I understood the whole koan, that terse Zen story, right there. *The branch of the plum facing south and the branch of the plum facing north.* A great gash opened. When they rang the bell to bow at the altar, I stood up and walked straight out the door, said hello to no one, and walked home.

The next day I left for Colorado. In the long ride through San Luis before we hit the Rockies I remembered almost forty years ago my husband and I had driven here and at nightfall slept out in sleeping bags under a cottonwood near the side of the road. I felt the gap of all these years, wished we had stayed married so we would have known each other through our thirties and forties and fifties. All weekend I felt that space between then and now, between the past and the present. And when I came home today from that good weekend of hiking in the Rockies and eating expensive lamb chops in a fancy restaurant, listening to a young twenty-five-year-old Korean violinist at the Aspen Music Festival play Aaron Copland so that you were sliced across the face of the violin along with the cat strings, I still woke this morning at home with a loneliness I had no words for, a beehive of lost thoughts in my head, a hard nut in my stomach, and I knew nothing had changed. I could not go into that studio or climb into the notebook, no matter where or what enticement I brewed up (of course, I could—I'm a thirty-five-year writing veteran) but I knew I had to be before being, in the cold, where you can't turn around or wiggle. (The Zennists call it putting a snake in a bamboo pole.)

So I drive over to where my friends are gathering to write, the early evening still full of light, still only two hours of rain in 150 days and fires raging up the tall crackling Ponderosas. As I drive, I'm listening to *Cutting for Stone* by Abraham Verghese. I knew him ten years ago when he lived in Houston and I wrote him about his first book, about AIDS in Tennessee. We wrote each other and then he visited my class. We lost touch. As I listen to the exotic medical story in Ethiopia unfold, I think, *Abraham, when I knew you, I didn't know you had these stories in you.* I feel so proud of him and think, *Can I find you now to tell you?*

I park my car on the ordinary street, get out on the blue pavement, and slam the door shut. Across the way by the Honda are three friends. I do not talk a lot but pinch and hug their granddaughter, who is visiting. We walk into the house with the glasses of water on the low coffee table, the Fig Newtons and the rice crackers. I spy a dish of chocolate squares but I do not take one.

I want these women to be writing at the same time I write, because I cannot write this alone. This is about emptiness, not the rich kind where writing and all things come from, but the empty time after you drop the bomb. You are the only one left and there is no one to talk to. Food is contaminated; water is worse, but to have no one to talk to is the worst of all.

I lived the first eighteen years of my life, wanting my mother, never having her, rarely talking to her. Across the vast space of this writing group I suddenly realize today is her birthday. She would have been ninety-five. She died three years ago. This is also Nelson Mandela's birthday. The sun did a revolution and the earth revolved and two people, one important to the world and one important to the whole universe of my childhood, came forth out of nowhere.

So this is it. I have been pregnant with zero and because of that I could not write. That place back in what some call the mystery. Where do we come from and where do we go?

People say art matters. It doesn't matter the way a cheese sandwich does or a hand to cross a street or a big looming building brings shade as you pass under it. What matters? Maybe these quiet people bending over notebooks, silent, but pouring words onto the page. Maybe words matter. Maybe I would have wanted to talk to my mother all those years ago, tell her about the science experiment we did in Mr. Berke's class. How water evaporated and then fogged glass, and so we made the water exist again. How Mr. Berke mattered terribly to me in fifth grade. I wanted, Mother, to tell you this, and what a sheet of paper with lines felt like against a small oak desk and my long legs under the desk. Mother, I had two hands. I had one thumb and fingers around a pen. I wanted to tell you all this.

Epilogue

◆ ◆ ◆

When the Buddha knew he was close to dying—he was in his eight-ies—he longed to see the town of Vaishali, with its many beautiful temples, one more time. He and his close disciple, Ananda, walked slow miles for a final visit, practicing meditation and mindfulness as they went, peaceful, not harming anything. This kind of slow walk-ing emits light, creates more time and space, so, though the Buddha was close to his end, he did not hurry. He had time to enjoy the air and sun, the trees he passed, the sounds of birds, the companion-ship of his old friend Ananda.

Just outside the city of Vaishali, he went into retreat for two weeks and it was then he decided he would die within three months. He came out of retreat, informed Ananda of this, and then stood on a hill overlooking Vaishali, never entering the city again. As he took Anan-da's arm it is said in the sutras he gazed at Vaishali for the last time with "the eyes of an elephant queen," then he turned and went on his way.

I have always been moved by this image and that moment. Think of the immensity and weight, the presence of a huge gray elephant—and a queen, no less. That kind of regal female vulner-ability, aware of the cycles of birth and death. This human being, this Awakened One, sustained that taut line between the poignant beauty of existence and the coincident knowledge of imperma-nence, that nothing is forever, you cannot hold on. Looking upon something you love at the same time knowing and accepting your death, turning to leave, saying good-bye.

> All things that manifest must pass
> Continue on with vigor
>
> —*last words of the Buddha*

Another story I carry close is about the French writer Colette. She met her third husband, Maurice Goudeket, a Jew, seventeen years her junior, when she was fifty-two, and married him ten years later.

When Maurice was a boy of sixteen, he came home from school for noon lunch and announced to his mother, *We learned today about the writer Colette. Someday I'm going to marry her.*

To give you an example of the French people's adoration of her writing: One evening when Colette, in her eighties, walked out of a small town theater, a thief snatched her purse. The next day the event was printed in the local papers. Soon after, her handbag was returned, all money intact, with a note: *I didn't know it was you.* She was loved even by the pickpockets.

When the Nazis took over Paris during World War II, Maurice was taken as part of their plan to exterminate all Jews. Colette went to the Vichy government demanding, beseeching his release. They told her they would see what they could do—not knowing where he was and if he'd already been deported.

She went home and sat by a window near the front door. During the hard weeks of uncertainty and fear while she waited in her chair, with pen in hand and paper on lap she wrote *Gigi,* the charming story of a young French girl growing up that eventually became a Broadway play and a Hollywood movie.

This is a tribute to the human imagination and spirit, its autonomy under terrible duress, its ability to shine forth—even to create. (And yes, Maurice was finally released.)

I tell my students, *Shut up and write.* These four words are all you need, but to realize them is not so easy. The phrase has the terseness of Zen—pithy, cutting through, to the point. But we have to fall through many layers of human life to directly meet its prescription. We have to know the dignity of language, the dimensions of war and aggression, then patience, the slow recording of detail, desire, anguish, hope, then letting go, silence and speech, imperturbability, resolve, then flummoxing, losing it all, thinking we can escape. We go through the whole gamut, the extremes, till we lower ourselves into the center— quiet, looking harmless, barely moving, but ferocious inside, determined, touching down on delight and candor, pouring it onto the page.

In ancient China a monk named Judi in Wu province practiced very hard alone. During a great rainstorm a nun named Shiji (Reality) arrived. She circled Judi three times and said, "If you can speak, I'll stay the night." He could think of no response. She left into the stormy dark. Judi lamented to himself, "I have no spirit. I could not even help this woman." He resolved to pack up his things and go to a monastery. That night in his sleep a mountain nymph came to him and whispered in his ear, *Wait. You do not need to leave this mountain, someone will come to you.* He woke, thought he'd just been dreaming, but decided he could postpone his journey for a month. On the tenth day, while he was sitting cross-legged in meditation in his hut, a great teacher arrived and sat opposite him. Judi, pleased, surprised, bowed and recounted his despair. The teacher raised one finger and pointed it at him. On the spot Judi experienced enlightenment.

From then on, all his life, whenever a monk approached him, Judi would raise a single finger, with no other explanation. It was an austere response but it contained multitudes.

Whenever I am asked in the last twenty-five years, what does it take? I repeat the same four words. It doesn't make for long conversation. The inquirer usually wants me to discuss the ins and outs, the romance of a writing life, to get lost in the many creases, shadows, and ripples, but that doesn't meet the mark. Yes, you do take the bounty of all that embellishment, that wanting and resistance, suffering and elation, but you drive it down that thin line of practice, that one step, one breath, one word at a time. On that narrow precipice you encounter yourself again and again, in love, in hate, in life, and in death. Please, join the ranks of the tried and true. Become a person of peace. When you practice, you stop causing trouble for everyone else. The trouble—the memories, the hurts, all of it—is now yours. You claim it; you are responsible. And you know what to do: *Shut up and write.*

There is a saying that the student must surpass the teacher for the teachings to continue to the next generation. Katagiri Roshi was one of the teachers who brought Zen out of the ancient Japanese monasteries and taught us what he knew. It's our responsibility to carry on the lineage. We who know American culture must make it vital, robust, and relevant right now so the seed may grow and take root. My great teacher has been dead for over twenty years. I want the teachings to sing through the ink of our pens and in the electric hum of our computers, to reveal freedom and understanding in our unique way. The Western world needed the Asian teachings, but Zen also needed us. I am standing on his shoulders.

Appendix 1

◆　◆　◆

Books Read for Retreats

In yearlong intensives students are assigned four books for each seasonal meeting. In two of the intensives I also asked them to read one book during the year that they always wanted to read but never got around to. I asked them to lean toward the classics.

Inside the Night Sky Intensive 2004

WINTER

Fugitive Pieces by Anne Michaels
Patrimony by Philip Roth
Push by Sapphire
The Triggering Town by Richard Hugo

SPRING

Ex Libris by Anne Fadiman
Newjack: Guarding Sing Sing by Ted Conover
The Spirit Catches You and You Fall Down by Anne Fadiman
Waiting by Ha Jin

SUMMER

Fierce Attachments by Vivian Gornick
Mitchell & Ruff: An American Profile in Jazz by William Zinsser

Montana 1948 by Larry Watson
Waiting for Snow in Havana by Carlos Eire

FALL

At the Bottom of the River by Jamaica Kincaid
Savage Beauty by Nancy Milford
The Black Notebooks by Toi Derricotte
The Things They Carried by Tim O'Brien

World Comes Home Intensive 2006

WINTER

Black Livingstone by Pagan Kennedy
Giovanni's Room by James Baldwin
Home Before Dark by Susan Cheever
John Cheever short stories: "Goodbye, My Brother"
                           "The Housebreaker of Shady Hill"
                           "The Enormous Radio"
                           "The Swimmer"

SPRING

A Place to Stand by Jimmy Santiago Baca
Bones of the Master by George Crane
The Language of Baklava by Diana Abu-Jaber
Walking with the Wind by John Lewis

SUMMER

Mockingbird by Charles J. Shields
The Song of the Lark by Willa Cather
Three Day Road by Joseph Boyden
To Kill a Mockingbird by Harper Lee

FALL

Candyfreak by Steve Almond
In Cold Blood by Truman Capote
Stoner by John Williams
The Amazing Adventures of Kavalier & Clay by Michael Chabon

Deep and Slow Intensive 2009

WINTER

Ceremony by Leslie Marmon Silko
Crooked Cucumber by David Chadwick
The Great Gatsby by F. Scott Fitzgerald
When the Emperor Was Divine by Julie Otsuka

SPRING

Departures by Paul Zweig
Heat by Bill Buford
Red Azalea by Anchee Min
The Brief Wondrous Life of Oscar Wao by Junot Díaz
The Situation and the Story by Vivian Gornick

SUMMER

America Is in the Heart by Carlos Bulosan
Miriam's Kitchen by Elizabeth Ehrlich
My Life in France by Julia Child
The Woman Warrior by Maxine Hong Kingston

FALL

Brothers and Keepers by John Edgar Wideman
Leaving Cheyenne by Larry McMurtry
Seeds from a Birch Tree by Clark Strand
The Florist's Daughter by Patricia Hampl

Intensive Reunion (February 2010)

A Gesture Life by Chang-Rae Lee
On Chesil Beach by Ian McEwan
Wide Sargasso Sea by Jean Rhys

Inside Out Intensive 2011

WINTER

Cheri, and The Last of Cheri by Colette
The Immortal Life of Henrietta Lacks by Rebecca Skloot
The Last Survivor by Timothy W. Ryback
Things Fall Apart by Chinua Achebe

SPRING

A Personal Matter by Kenzaburō Ōe
Just Kids by Patti Smith
King Leopold's Ghost by Adam Hochschild
The Old Man and the Sea by Ernest Hemingway

SPRING

Bearing Witness by Bernie Glassman
Contemporary Creative Nonfiction: I & Eye an anthology
        by Bich Minh Nguyen and Porter Shreve
Tortilla Curtain by T.C. Boyle
Choose one of these:
        Seabiscuit by Laura Hillenbrand or
        Unbroken by Laura Hillenbrand or
        The Spirit Catches You and You Fall Down by Anne Fadiman

FALL

Night by Elie Wiesel
Reflections in a Golden Eye by Carson McCullers

*We Wish to Inform You That Tomorrow We Will Be Killed with
        Our Families* by Philip Gourevitch
New Yorker articles by Philip Gourevitch:
        "Letter from Rwanda," July 11/18, 2001
        "Reporter at Large: The Life After," May 4, 2009

Intensive Reunion (February 2012)

The Makioka Sisters by Junichiro Tanizaki

Following are books read during the last twelve years in single-week True Secret Retreats. Usually only one or two books are assigned, not because it is less rigorous than intensives but because there is a different intention—to experience the interconnectedness of the sitting, walking, and writing and to taste a feeling of space and peace. (Students who attend any True Secret Retreats usually had to have studied with me before in a writing workshop.)

The Lone Ranger and Tonto Fistfight in Heaven by Sherman Alexie
Death Comes to the Archbishop by Willa Cather
The House on Mango Street by Sandra Cisneros
Breath, Eyes, Memory by Edwidge Danticat
The Paperboy by Pete Dexter
Chronicles by Bob Dylan
A Lesson Before Dying by Ernest J. Gaines
The Honey Thief by Elizabeth Graver
Praying for Sheetrock by Melissa Fay Greene
Dharma, Color, and Culture by Hilda Gutiérrez Baldoquín
Being Peace by Thich Nhat Hanh
Death in the Afternoon by Ernest Hemingway
31 Letters and 13 Dreams: Poems by Richard Hugo
A Child Out of Alcatraz by Tara Ison
Gardening at the Dragon's Gate by Wendy Johnson

Survival in Auschwitz by Primo Levi
Edge of Taos Desert by Mabel Dodge Luhan
West with the Night by Beryl Markham
Under the Tuscan Sun by Frances Mayes
The Ballad of the Sad Café by Carson McCullers
Leaving Cheyenne by Larry McMurtry
The Last Picture Show by Larry McMurtry
So Long, See You Tomorrow by William Maxwell
House Made of Dawn by N. Scott Momaday
Becoming a Man by Paul Monette
Borrowed Time by Paul Monette
Running in the Family by Michael Ondaatje
The Work of This Moment by Toni Packer
Close Range: Wyoming Stories by Annie Proulx
Hunger of Memory by Richard Rodriguez
The Human Stain by Philip Roth
Street Zen by David Schneider
The Delicacy and Strength of Lace
        by Leslie Marmon Silko and James Wright
Crossing to Safety by Wallace Stegner
Subtle Sound by Maurine Stuart
Zen Mind, Beginner's Mind by Shunryu Suzuki
Seven Japanese Tales by Junichiro Tanizaki
At Hell's Gate by Claude Anshin Thomas
The Farm on the River of Emeralds by Moritz Thomsen
Living Poor by Moritz Thomsen
Cutting Through Spiritual Materialism by Chögyam Trungpa Rinpoche
My Own Country by Abraham Verghese

Appendix 2

◆ ◆ ◆

Volunteer Jobs

Each job has its own sheet of paper. I want you to be able to envision and duplicate whatever you need for a retreat. So I give this to you.

Lighting Candles
(candles are on the altar and in two niches built into the wall)

Monday   _____

Tuesday   _____

Wednesday   _____

Thursday   _____

Friday   _____

Saturday   _____

(Light candles before each session in the schedule)

Snuffing Candles

Monday   _____

Tuesday   _____

Wednesday   _____

Thursday   _____

Friday   _____

Saturday   _____

(Snuff candles at the end of each session.)

Filling Water Pitchers
(Students take a paper cup and put their name on it so it can be used throughout the week.)

Monday   _____

Tuesday   _____

Wednesday   _____

Thursday   _____

Friday   _____

Saturday   _____

Sweeping Zendo

Monday P.M. _____

Tuesday A.M. _____ Tuesday P.M. _____

Wednesday A.M. _____ Wednesday P.M. _____

Thursday A.M. _____ Thursday P.M. _____

Friday A.M. _____ Friday P.M. _____

Saturday A.M. _____

Sweeping Porch

Monday P.M. _____

Tuesday A.M. _____ Tuesday P.M. _____

Wednesday A.M. _____ Wednesday P.M. _____

Thursday A.M. _____ Thursday P.M. _____

Friday A.M. _____ Friday P.M. _____

Saturday A.M. _____

Leading Silent Reading Group

Monday   _____

Tuesday   _____

Wednesday   _____

Thursday   _____

Friday   _____

Saturday   _____

Ringing Morning Bell for the 7:30 A.M. Sit

Monday   _____

Tuesday   _____

Wednesday   _____

Thursday   _____

Friday   _____

Saturday   _____

Town Crier

Monday   _____

Tuesday   _____

Wednesday   _____

Thursday   _____

Friday   _____

Saturday   _____

Permissions Acknowledgments

◆ ◆ ◆

Acknowledgments

◆   ◆   ◆

A deep thank you to Maria Fortin, who supported and helped envision all my programs at the Mabel Dodge Lujan House for the last twenty years, including, of course, the True Secret retreats.

And much appreciation to John Dear and his tireless work for peace.

ABOUT THE AUTHOR

NATALIE GOLDBERG is a poet, painter, teacher, and the author of twelve books, including *Writing Down the Bones: Freeing the Writer Within* (which has sold more than 1.5 million copies and has been translated into fourteen languages) and *Old Friend from Far Away: The Practice of Writing Memoir*. She has taught seminars and led retreats for thirty-five years to people from around the world, and lives in northern New Mexico.